WALKING COUNTRY

NIDDERDALE

Paul Hannon

D1313219

HILLSIDE GUIDES - ACROSS THE NORTH

Long Distance Walks
- COAST TO COAST WALK
- DALES WAY
- CLEVELAND WAY
- WESTMORLAND WAY
- FURNESS WAY
- CUMBERLAND WAY
- LADY ANNE'S WAY
- NORTH BOWLAND TRAVERSE

Circular Walks - Peak District
- NORTHERN PEAK
- EASTERN PEAK
- CENTRAL PEAK
- SOUTHERN PEAK
- WESTERN PEAK

Circular Walks - Lancashire
- BOWLAND
- PENDLE & THE RIBBLE

Circular Walks - Yorkshire Dales
- HOWGILL FELLS
- THREE PEAKS
- MALHAMDALE
- WHARFEDALE
- NIDDERDALE
- WENSLEYDALE
- SWALEDALE

Circular Walks - North York Moors
- WESTERN MOORS
- SOUTHERN MOORS
- NORTHERN MOORS

Circular Walks - South Pennines
- BRONTE COUNTRY
- CALDERDALE
- ILKLEY MOOR

Circular Walks - North Pennines
- TEESDALE
- EDEN VALLEY

Hillwalking - Lake District
- OVER LAKELAND MOUNTAINS
- OVER LAKELAND FELLS

Yorkshire Pub Walks
- HARROGATE/WHARFE VALLEY
- HAWORTH/AIRE VALLEY

Large format colour hardback
FREEDOM OF THE DALES

BIKING COUNTRY
- YORKSHIRE DALES CYCLE WAY
- WEST YORKSHIRE CYCLE WAY
- MOUNTAIN BIKING - WEST & SOUTH YORKSHIRE
- AIRE VALLEY BIKING GUIDE
- CALDERDALE BIKING GUIDE
- GLASGOW Clyde Valley & Loch Lomond

- YORK WALKS Theme Walks around the historic city

- WALKING COUNTRY TRIVIA QUIZ

Send for a detailed list and current prices

WALKING COUNTRY

NIDDERDALE

Paul Hannon

HILLSIDE

HILLSIDE
PUBLICATIONS
11 Nessfield Grove
Keighley
West Yorkshire
BD22 6NU

First published 1985
Revised and extended 1994
5th impression 1997

© Paul Hannon 1985, 1997

ISBN 1 870141 23 7

Cover illustration: Guise Cliff, above Pateley Bridge
Back cover: Gouthwaite; Brimham Rocks; Fountains Abbey
(Paul Hannon/Big Country Picture Library)

Printed in Great Britain by
Carnmor Print and Design
95-97 London Road
Preston
Lancashire
PR1 4BA

CONTENTS

INTRODUCTION

Though far from least attractive of the Yorkshire Dales, Nidderdale is probably the least known of the major ones. Certainly the gateways of Harrogate and Knareborough receive their share of attention, but more glamorous neighbours Wharfedale and Wensleydale siphon off most visitors. This leaves Nidderdale free from congestion, and leaves the rambler 'free' to roam, often in solitude. If anything Nidderdale has taken a step backwards in recent years, for both its youth hostels, at Dacre Banks and Ramsgill, were closed in the 1980s, resulting in thousands of lost visitors - predominantly walkers - every year.

In spite of this solitude, Nidderdale is renowned far and wide for a handful of attractions, notably the vastly differing natural features of Brimham Rocks and How Stean Gorge. Further up-dale are the holes of Goyden Pot and Manchester Hole, while at the dale head are the reservoirs of Scar House and Angram, in an extremely bleak setting overshadowed by the highest fells. Add to this Gouthwaite Reservoir, Yorke's Folly and Guise Cliff, the sleepy villages of Ramsgill and Wath, and we are now scratching the surface.

Little Whernside across Scar House Reservoir

Aside from natural rockscapes and man-made lakes, Nidderdale boasts two other outstanding aspects - heather and trees. The valley is little short of lavished with attractive woodland, while the heather moors reach endlessly over sweeping horizons. In the upper dale, much of this vast moorland is managed for grouse shooting, which makes us grateful indeed for the rights of way that criss-cross the higher ground.

Jenny Twigg and Her Daughter Tib, above Ramsgill

The area might be divided into three sections, namely the well defined upper valley north of Pateley Bridge; the Nidd Valley itself, downstream; and the country reaching towards Ripon. The moors that form Nidderdale's eastern boundary fall equally attractively to this rolling landscape, where tidy villages are scattered amongst the sylvan charms of the youthful rivers Skell, Laver and Burn. Though these all flow into the lower Ure rather than the Nidd, this area is very much part of the whole scene. Here we find much rich parkland, and the finest individual feature this side of York, namely the incomparable Fountains Abbey and attendant Studley Royal estate. The inclusion of this adjacent area is not merely for convenience, for historically upper Nidderdale had far stronger links with the Kirkby Malzeard to Ripon district than with the Harrogate area much further down the valley. In monastic times, the high moors dividing the two saw a busy passage of trade as monks trod their way over to markets at Kirkby Malzeard and to Masham and Fountains Abbey itself, laden with the fruits of their labours, often in the form of lead or wool. Before passing to the abbeys of Fountains and Byland, the whole of Nidderdale was a Royal hunting chase.

Virtually all this guide falls within the bounds of the Nidderdale Area of Outstanding Natural Beauty (designated in 1994), a fully merited if belated recognition of the exceptional scenic qualities of this landscape. Unjust exclusion from the Yorkshire Dales National Park at its formation - certainly in the case of the dale above Pateley Bridge, at least - was largely due to some less than enthusiastic landowning interests: one visit to this last major valley at the east side of the Yorkshire Dales will confirm, however, it concedes nothing to its National Park neighbours.

Pateley Bridge - *Kenaresforde* in Domesday - is a busy little town, the undisputed 'capital' of Nidderdale. It draws from far and wide: to Nidderdale folk it is the hub of dale life, to visitors from further afield, the first stop. It is literally the key to the upper dale, for all intent on exploring these finest, wilder reaches will pass through here first. Within the town itself are inns and cafes; an information centre; buses down-dale to Harrogate; a riverside park; innumerable shops, some hidden down inviting narrow alleys; and the award-winning Nidderdale Museum. On display here are over 4000 items of life gone by. Unfortunately most of Pateley's industry comes within its scope, for at one time railways, quarrying and lead mining could be added to the more permanent farming. At Pateley, too, there is always the river: the Nidd's green banks carry paths in both directions, and here, many years ago, the author saw his first kingfisher.

Fallow deer, Ripley Park

8

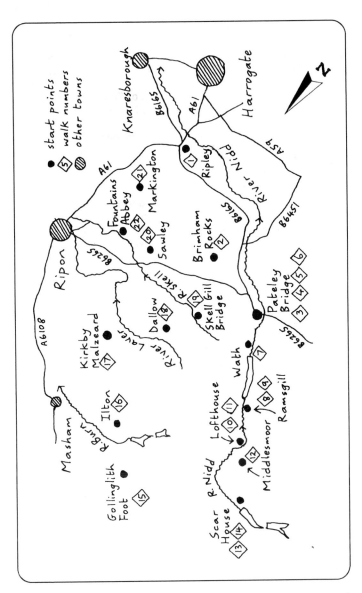

Getting around

Public transport to and within the area is at best mixed. Services radiate from either Harrogate or Ripon. From Harrogate buses up the Nidd Valley serve Pateley Bridge, while services between Harrogate and Ripon reach some of the villages east of the Nidd. Quite a number of walks have no public transport, but many of those in Upper Nidderdale have Summer Sunday buses. Only 1 of the 22 walks is described as a linear ramble, though permutations can be created by linking different sections, with careful planning. The only rail line in the area is that serving Harrogate, only of use in reaching the district.

Using the guide

Each walk is self-contained, with essential information being followed by a simple map and concise description of the route. Dovetailed between this are useful notes of features along the way, and interspersed are illustrations which both capture the flavour of the walks and document the many items of interest. The instructions are made easier to follow by the essential route description being in bold type.

The simple sketch maps identify the location of the routes rather than the fine detail, and whilst the route description should be sufficient to guide you around, an Ordnance Survey map is recommended: the route can easily be plotted on the relevant one. To gain the most from a walk, the remarkable detail of the 1:25,000 scale maps cannot be matched. They also serve to vary walks as desired, giving an improved picture of one's surroundings and the availability of linking paths. 1997 saw publication of a new OS map *Explorer 27 - Nidderdale*, and this one sheet covers all but three of the walks in their entirety. The following two sheets serve the overlaps:

Outdoor Leisure 30 - Yorkshire Dales North/Central: 13;14;15
Pathfinder 630 - Middleham & Jervaulx Abbey: 15
(the latter map will be replaced by an Explorer map in due course)

Additionally, ideal for general planning purposes are Landranger maps at the scale of 1:50,000, and all but three walks are found on one map, *99 - Northallerton & Ripon*. Walks 13 and 14 overlap onto *98 - Wensleydale & Upper Wharfedale* and Walk 1 onto *104 - Leeds, Bradford & Harrogate*.

SOME USEFUL ADDRESSES

Ramblers' Association
1/5 Wandsworth Road, London SW8 2XX
Tel. 0171-339 8500

Pateley Bridge Tourist Information
14 High Street, Pateley Bridge HG3 5AW
Tel. 01423-711147
(seasonal opening)

Harrogate Tourist Information
Royal Baths Assembly Rooms
Crescent Road, Harrogate HG1 2RR
Tel. 01423-525666

Ripon Tourist Information
Minster Road, Ripon HG4 1LT
Tel. 01765-604625
(seasonal opening)

Yorkshire Dales Society
Otley Civic Centre, Cross Green, Otley LS21 1HD
Tel. 01943-461938

The National Trust
Regional Office
Goddards, 27 Tadcaster Road, York YO2 2QG
Tel. 01904-702021

British Rail
Harrogate - Tel. (Leeds) 0113-244 8133

Bus operators
Harrogate & District Travel Tel. 01423-566061
for Nidderdale area

United Bus Company (Darlington) Tel. 01325-468771
for Ripon area

THE NIDD VALLEY

START Ripley   Grid ref. SE 284605

FINISH Summerbridge   **DISTANCE** 8¼ miles

ORDNANCE SURVEY MAPS
1:50,000
Landranger 99 - Northallerton & Ripon
Landranger 104 - Leeds, Bradford & Harrogate
1:25,000
Explorer 26 - Nidderdale

ACCESS Start from the market cross outside the *Boars Head* in the village centre. Large car park at the village entrance. Served by Harrogate-Ripon buses, and an occasional Harrogate-Pateley Bridge bus. Summerbridge is served by the regular Pateley Bridge service from Harrogate as well as the occasional one.

Ripley exudes character and breathes history. It was a market town in 1357, and has been the manorial seat of the Ingilby family since before that. Nothing here is without interest, though the castle is the major attraction. First sight is the imposing gatehouse, dating from the early 15th century. Through its great arch are spacious lawns and a courtyard. The castle itself was largely rebuilt in 1555, and much enlarged in 1780, though the old tower is less than a century after the gatehouse.

After the battle of Marston Moor this Royalist castle supposedly received a visit from Oliver Cromwell, while his troops shot Royalist prisoners they had brought to the village. The lakes and deer park were laid out by Capability Brown, these magnificent grounds being open from April to October. The castle itself is also open at various times in this period, including all weekends, and is well worth a visit for both its splendid interior and the contents within.

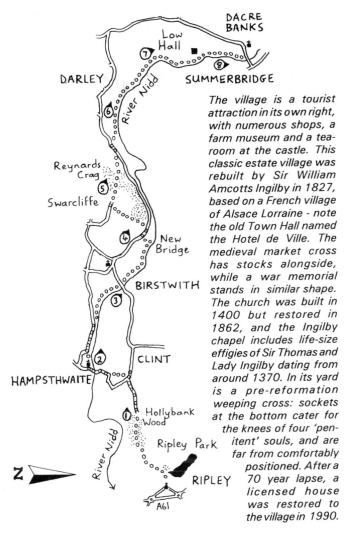

The village is a tourist attraction in its own right, with numerous shops, a farm museum and a tea-room at the castle. This classic estate village was rebuilt by Sir William Amcotts Ingilby in 1827, based on a French village of Alsace Lorraine - note the old Town Hall named the Hotel de Ville. The medieval market cross has stocks alongside, while a war memorial stands in similar shape. The church was built in 1400 but restored in 1862, and the Ingilby chapel includes life-size effigies of Sir Thomas and Lady Ingilby dating from around 1370. In its yard is a pre-reformation weeping cross: sockets at the bottom cater for the knees of four 'penitent' souls, and are far from comfortably positioned. After a 70 year lapse, a licensed house was restored to the village in 1990.

□ **Head along the road between the church and the castle, quickly becoming rougher as it crosses Ripley Beck and rises outside the castle grounds.** During the rise there is a good view

Ripley Cross

back to the castle itself. **When the park wall turns right remain on the track straight ahead,** though an early diversion up the wall-side track gives a glimpse of the deer within the park. **Continuing on, bear right when a farm track goes left, and our way continues as a superb cart track rising to enter Hollybank Wood.**

These glorious woodlands are perhaps at their finest in Spring, when carpeted with bluebells. **At Holly Bank Lodge a surfaced lane runs serenely on to the road at Clint.** A detour a mere hundred yards up the road finds the base of the ancient Clint Cross, restored in 1977, and adjacent stocks.

The way, meanwhile, crosses straight over the road to a stile, and follows the left-hand wall away. On the brow there is a grand prospect of the verdant Nidd Valley, including much of the route. With the solid tower of Hampsthwaite church prominent below, **descend by the field boundary to meet the corner of a road** at the site of a former bridge on the defunct Nidd Valley Railway. This is the first of many signs of the old line to be encountered, for it shadows much of the route in close proximity to the river. The branch railway ran from Nidd Bridge, near Harrogate to Pateley Bridge, being opened in 1862 and fully closed in 1964. **Head straight along the road, over the narrow bridge** - rebuilt in 1640 - **across the Nidd and on towards the church. The village centre is just ahead up Church Lane.**

Once a busy market town, it also marked an important river crossing for the Romans on their road from Ilkley across to Aldborough, near Boroughbridge.

Clint Cross

14

A path however turns through the church gate, along the front and on to a gate at the far end. The church of St Thomas a 'Becket dates largely from only a century ago, though the tower is a good 500 years old. *Here a gem of a green byway (part-flagged) runs between hedgerows to emerge on the up-dale road.* From hereon the walk coincides with the route of the Nidderdale Way, and all signs pertaining to it are therefore of use to us. *Go right for a few minutes until a part-ruinous stable block, then from the gate behind enter a field. A slim path bears across the pasture to approach the river to commence following it upstream. When a wooded bank deflects the path from the river, keep straight on to the yard of the busy Birstwith feed mill.* A recent diversion takes the path round the outside to join the road in Birstwith.

Hampsthwaite Bridge

With the river bridge and inn to the right, and attractive corners to the left, **the walk crosses straight over and along a short-lived cut to rejoin the river.** Look up to the left to see the proud spire of Birstwith church (1857), and on the hill above the grand sight of Swarcliffe Hall (1848) in its lovely grounds. **Running along the edge of the sports fields the path remains near the Nidd until arrival at the shapely arch of New Bridge.** Dating from around 1615, it was on the packhorse route from Ripon to Skipton, but was demolished in 1822 and rebuilt 25 yards downstream.

15

Having had a look, turn back up the hedgerowed lane to the left to rise to a drive between a house bearing a 1688 datestone and a farm. Climb to meet the road, and turn right for a few minutes on a gradual descent with outstanding wooded scenery over the valley, and barely a dwellings in sight. *Locate a part-hidden stile on the left and climb the field-side to enter a wood, a grand path climbing stiffly along the edge of the plantation.* Towards the top look for fine views back over the Birstwith neighbourhood. *At the top a drive is joined and followed up onto a lane.*

New Bridge

Go right, enjoying views up-dale to the great curve of the valley with higher moors beyond. *At the lane's early demise, go through the gate but avoid a slaughterers by turning down a wooded green way to the right. A better path forms to drop past a pond and through a gate into the wood of Reynards Crag. Substantially flagged if sometimes poorly drained, it leads down through some glorious birchwood. At a small clearing by a corner of the wood, the bridleway continues down to the road, while a left fork runs a short way on to curve round to a part-hidden stile out of the trees. Cross straight over a couple of fields parallel with the road below, then along a wall-side to a gate, crossing to a stile to emerge onto the road.*

Go left past the thatched Holme Hall, known as Darley Laundry, which it operated as at the end of the 19th century. *Beyond the few dwellings on this outskirt of Darley* (continue straight on for the pub) *take a stile on the right to drop diagonally down a big field to the far corner. From a stile a path squeezes along the top of a wooded bank then drops to a muddy farm bridge over a beck.*

16

Ignoring a footbridge on the right and the old railway beneath the sewage works on the left, adhere to the improving riverbank for a grand stroll. Beyond a footbridge the garden foots of new prestige dwellings are crossed on the site of the former Darley railway station, *then the path follows a particularly lovely section of riverbank curving around a large sheep pasture. A footbridge towards the end crosses a side beck, and the walk continues, unfailingly along the bank towards Summerbridge.*

Features en route are, inevitably, the embankment of the old line; then for some time the prospect of Low Hall's splendid facade over to the left (some stones in this Tudor-style house are said to have come from Fountains Abbey); and also nice views of the wooded slopes rising to Brimham Rocks above Summerbridge. **The path is restricted a little too zealously by a fence for some considerable time, but the way remains pleasant all the way to the extensive and well tended sports fields of Dacre Banks, to reach the arched bridge dividing the two communities.** *Ahead is a busy sawmill, where wood arrives from all over to be prepared largely for use in furniture. Both Dacre Banks and Summerbridge offer licensed premises, while the latter even boasts a chip shop.*

The Gatehouse,
Ripley Castle

17

2

BRIMHAM ROCKS

START Brimham Rocks   Grid ref. SE 208645

DISTANCE 5 miles

ORDNANCE SURVEY MAPS
1:50,000
Landranger 99 - Northallerton & Ripon
1:25,000
Explorer 26 - Nidderdale

ACCESS Start from the large National Trust car park at the main entrance to Brimham Rocks. Fell Beck or Smelthouses make useful alternative starts, thus placing the highlight of the journey midway: if coming by bus, then they are really obligatory starts. The Harrogate-Pateley Bridge bus runs through Low Laithe, just down a rough lane from Smelthouses; an occasional Ripon-Pateley Bridge bus serves Fell Beck.

Brimham Rocks are the pride of Nidderdale, and deservedly regarded as its most famous visitor attraction. The surrounding countryside, however, is also of the highest standard, as this excursion will readily prove.

☐ *From the car park a broad carriageway leads directly to Brimham House. This gets the walk off to a proper start, saving the attractions of the intervening wonderland for journey's end. Otherwise, turn off from the car park information board where a well-made path heads right into the heart of things: countless offshoots set forth to discover other hidden delights, eventually re-emerging near the house.* Formerly the 'Rocks House', it was built in 1792 by Lord Grantley for his moor keeper. It now serves as a shop and information point, with all the usual National Trust aromas. Refreshments and toilets are also in evidence.

Leaving these opening attractions for a possible re-run at the end, take the main path round to the left of the house. Further splendid outcrops are encountered, including some of the better known such as the Dancing Bear (immediately) and Idol Rock. *Beyond the last rocks the path loops back to the right: here leave it by a narrow green path which maintains the northerly aim and drops down to join a wider path. Turn left on it, and keeping left at a fork it leads onto a parallel farm drive on the moor-edge.*

The Dancing Bear

Double back left on this rough road, passing through woods to approach Brimham Rocks Farm (High North Pasture Farm on maps). Before it, however, leave the drive at the first gate (two awkwardly together, in fact) on the right after the trees. Cross to a gateway at the far end, then on again to a gate in the far right corner, in front of North Pasture Farm. Enter the yard by another gate, and leave by one on the left after the main buildings.

Bear right across the field to locate a stile in a fence by a tiny stream. Continue straight on to a gate at the head of a green lane. Turn down it between enclosing walls, remaining on its pleasant course (and ignoring a branch right) as it winds down to cross Fell Beck before rising to the Ripon road. Descend left to the hamlet of Fell Beck, passing (or not) the **Half Moon inn**, *the setting for a harvest festival each September.*

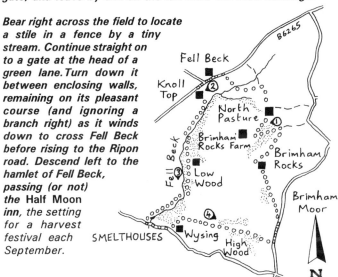

Continue up the road as it climbs away, just as far as the first farm road to the left. Pass between the buildings of Knoll Top to a gate, then swing right to a stile. Descend wall-side to another stile, then turn right above the beck to a gateway. Now a clearer path through the trees remains well above the beck as far as the next fence: from the left-hand of two stiles it drops to accompany the beck above a dam and a weir, as far as a walled track from the right. Here double back left down to a footbridge, remaining in the wood by turning right on a gradually rising path.

On approaching a walled enclosure the path forks: turn down to the right (without entering the field), the path soon continuing on the level to leave the trees at a stile below the isolated buildings of Low Wood. A thin path heads away to join a wider one descending from the left. Ignore a branch down to the beck, but remain level on a super green way to enter deep birchwoods. The path eventually meets another, just past a stile. Follow it down to the right to a footbridge, and trace the beck downstream to emerge onto the lane through Smelthouses.

Smelthouses is a charming hamlet in a setting to match. A rich assortment of graceful dwellings stand near the beck, where as early as the 14th century ore was brought from the lead mines

Idol Rock

20

for smelting by the monks of Fountains Abbey. These were joined by several flax mills, including possibly the earliest in the district, in 1798. It is now difficult to imagine that this sequestered spot was ever a hive of activity.

The Druid's Writing Desk

Turn left over the bridge, and continue a short way up the road as far as a drive on the left at Wysing House. Already the Rocks skyline is evident. Just past the attractive range of buildings at Low Wood House, the track swings left; here leave it by a gate on the right to follow a wide green track rising very gradually. This is a 'real' green byway, unviolated by motors, a natural corridor: it is also a former Monks' trod, one of the cross-country trade routes radiating from Fountains Abbey. **Mostly enclosed, it later follows a fence to arrive at a gate where High Wood comes up to meet us. Beyond a gate a path heads up through the pasture to a gateway in the wall on the right, then soon leaves the trees to rise to the left. Through another gateway and along a fieldside, typical Brimham country is now dominant on the left. One more gate is met before emerging onto the road.**

Heading left onto Brimham Moor, the drive back to the Rocks car park leaves the road to finish the walk, though an earlier fork sees a branch remain on the moor to escape the road a little earlier. Time to go exploring again!

3

PANORAMA WALK

START Pateley Bridge   Grid ref. SE 157655

DISTANCE 5 miles

ORDNANCE SURVEY MAPS
1:50,000
Landranger 99 - Northallerton & Ripon
1:25,000
Explorer 26 - Nidderdale

ACCESS Town centre car parks; bus service from Harrogate.

Largely a riverside walk, but with a start that lives up to its name.

☐ *From the bridge at the foot of the High Street head up the main thoroughfare, swinging right at the top to quickly level out. After about 150 yards an urban footpath sign points up a flight of steps to the start of the Panorama Walk. A steep, enclosed tarmac path climbs past an inscribed stone tablet above a well.* Early views updale back over the church tower find Great Whernside already slotting in on the horizon. **Beyond the entrance to the cemetery a snicket offers a detour along to the old church.** En route are wide views over Bewerley Moor and Gouthwaite Reservoir beyond the gravestones. Embowered in greenery in high altitude seclusion, the roofless church of St. Mary dates from the 13th century. It was replaced by the parish church of St. Cuthbert in the 19th century, and saved from complete ruin as a sister's memorial to her brother in 1906.

Glasshouses Church

Back on the main route the gradient soon eases and the way remains surfaced, enabling the views to be appreciated effortlessy. Part-way along, an iron gate admits to a traditional viewing station on a craggy knoll. The Panorama Walk is, not surprisingly, a popular local promenade, and though most Nidderdale walks offer extensive views, none are as easily accessible to all. Probably the finest feature is the prospect of Guise Cliff directly across the valley, with Yorke's Folly silhouetted. **On reaching the tidy hamlet of Knott, the track widens into a lane to drop down onto the main road.** During this descent there are good views to Brimham Rocks serrating the skyline to the left, while down-dale Summerbridge nestles amidst rich natural woodland.

Two minutes along the footway to the left, cross to a kissing-gate just past a solitary dwelling. A flagged path leads down to a second field, to descend to a rough lane on the edge of Glasshouses. Turn left a short way, then past an attractive terrace head down a very steep flagged snicket providing a short-cut towards the river. Glasshouses village is an innoccuous settlement based around a spacious, sloping green: dominant feature is the church spire, prominent in many a local scene. The village owes much of its existence to the Metcalfe family, who erected housing and public buildings in the mid-19th century for the workers in their great flax spinning mill.

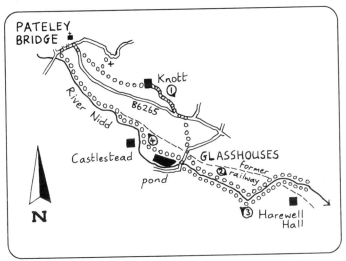

Rejoining the road, continue down past the former railway station and school to approach Glasshouses Bridge. The walk returns to this point after a further 2¼ miles downstream, so if a short-cut is required, just pick up the route on the near bank and head upstream.

Looking across the Nidd to Guise Cliff, from the Panorama Walk

Otherwise, turn before the bridge into the large millyard on the left, bearing right immediately after the main building. This substantial old mill now serves myriad operations, and its impressive riverside frontage is well seen from the return on the opposite bank. *Passing down the side of it a track descends towards the river. The way now clings to its bank, past the remains of an old viaduct to arrive at a wooden footbridge.*

The former railway line to Pateley Bridge is much in evidence on this walk, and the forlorn viaduct's supports are a particularly sad reminder of must have been a typical rural branch line. The Nidd Valley Line was opened in 1862 by the North Eastern Railway, largely to serve industry in the dale. It ran from Nidd Bridge near Harrogate to Pateley Bridge, and its single-track line finally succumbed in 1964, having already been closed to passengers 13 years earlier.

Glasshouses Mill

At the footbridge finally cross the river and turn upstream, clinging once more to the riverbank. *The farm up to the left is Harewell Hall, built by the influential Ingilby family in 1652.* **After the other section of viaduct, two sewage works are passed, though with eyes fixed on the river's wooded banks this is a minor inconvenience. Soon Glasshouses' singularly unglamorous bridge is reached. Cross it and take the broad carriageway upstream for an infallible return to Pateley Bridge.**

At once the drive is sandwiched between a mill cut and a big millpond, now a haven for bird-life. *Further, a nursery and the big house of Castlestead - erected in 1862 by the Metcalfes - are passed as* **the river is regained at a weir, to be traced upstream on a partly surfaced path.** *A branch path to Harefield Hall (another large house, now devoted to serving hungry and thirsty public) is passed, and* **the course of the railway line is in evidence during the final attractive stages before re-entering the town alongside a linear car park.**

The old church of St Mary, Pateley Bridge

YORKE'S FOLLY

START Pateley Bridge   Grid ref. SE 157655

DISTANCE 7 miles

ORDNANCE SURVEY MAPS
1:50,000
Landranger 99 - Northallerton & Ripon
1:25,000
Explorer 26 - Nidderdale

ACCESS Town centre car parks; bus service from Harrogate. An alternative start from Bewerley saves about a mile.

The first-time visitor will find the mix of woodland, beck, moorland and rock scenery unbelievable in such a compact area, and on a sunny September day he will be overawed by the heady colours.

☐ ***Cross the bridge at the foot of the High Street.*** *Note the grounds of Bewerley Park on the left, where the prestigious Nidderdale Show (a continuation of the Feast of St Mary, dating from 1320 when a market charter was granted) is held in September, and a regular local auction mart throughout the year. The hall itself, then seat of the Yorke family, was rebuilt in 1820 but demolished a century later. The Yorke name crops up throughout Nidderdale, incidentally, after their acquisition of the estates of Byland Abbey at the Dissolution. On the right is the attractive and much patronised public park.* ***Follow the road along to the edge of town - more properly known as Bridgehouse Gate - where a back road goes left to Bewerley.***

This is a hugely attractive village with carefully tended gardens leading the eye to innumerable cosy cottages. ***At the first junction double back to the right on a lane climbing out. After a couple of minutes take a stile on the left opposite a barn. Head***

27

directly up the field, through a collapsed wall to the top, there being deflected right to a gap-stile. A left turn here descends to enter Fishpond Wood via a kissing-gate. A path heads into the heart of the wood alongside a tiny stream which is crossed by a plank bridge before reaching the shore of the pond. *This ornamental lake is rather overgrown but not without attraction.*

On leaving its bank the path meets a wider track, turn right on it to swing round to a wicket-gate alongside a lane. Turn right along it, crossing Raven's Gill and then spiralling steeply uphill. As Skrikes Wood ends on the left, take a gate and rise steeply through bracken up the wall-side outside the trees, stiles leading through two further fields onto a farm road at Raven's Nest. Go left a few yards and then head up the shooters' track past the farm buildings, to run with a fence along the edge of Low Moor. To the left across Raven's Gill, the towers of Yorke's Folly wait patiently. 100 yards beyond a gate, as a wall takes over, turn left down a grassy path through heather to descend to gain Raven's Gill at a sheepfold and waterfall: *an idyllic spot.*

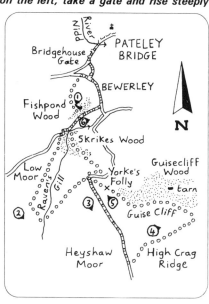

Across, a thin path slants left out of the gill, fading at a few outcrops leading to a sturdy boundary wall. Turn right along it, and at the second very substantial boundary stone a 'nonexistant' stile crosses to Nought Moor on the other side (one could alternatively follow the wall up to the road). Bear half-right away through the heather to join the moor road at the top of Nought Bank: *this was on the main road to Otley two centuries ago.* There are likely to be several cars parked around the lay-by for easy access to Yorke's Folly.

To this point the walk will return, but for now turn right up the lane for a gently rising march up to Heyshaw Moor. After little short of a mile, at last leave by a stile on the left. A clear way heads off to the outcrops and Ordnance column on High Crag Ridge, awash in a sea of bracken and heather. Less boldly the path runs on towards a TV mast, keeping well to the left of an extensive former quarry.

Without entering its confines go left of the mast's enclosure, to a stile above the exposed beginnings of Guise Cliff. Below is a wonderful panorama of the dale, seen as on a map beyond the magnificent rock architecture. Children and vertigo sufferers should NOT be near the edge, not only for the all too obvious sheer drop (which falls a good hundred feet at its peak) but because there are also some mischievous crevices. The blanket of woodland below is so complete as to hide the still waters of the oval Guisecliff Tarn in its midst.

The path runs unerringly left along the crest, and tempting branches seek out even more exposed situations. Soon a wall comes in to halt the fun, and the path runs on the moor edge to the waiting towers of Yorke's Folly. Highly prominent in many a Nidderdale scene, it was built around 200 years ago by a member of the Yorke family in order to provide employment. Supposed to resemble a Rhineland ruin, it does more so since one of the three original towers fell victim to a severe storm in 1893, at once rendering its local name of the Three Stoops redundant.

On Guise Cliff, looking over Guisecliff Wood to Glasshouses

29

Beyond, the path descends gradually but quickly to the road on Nought Bank. This time take the gate at the lay-by, and while a direct path descends at once, opt for one to the right. It winds round to the prominent Crocodile Rock: the resemblence is not obvious, but the location can't be challenged, while Elton John fans are likely to break into song at this point.

Yorke's Folly

The path then swings left around the moor to run round to a stile, where it winds down enchantingly into the top of Skrikes Wood. This magnificent wood has been designated a Nature Reserve chiefly for the variety of bird-life it attracts. **The main path descends left through the wood, emerging onto the road near the start of the walk.**

Turn right along it below Fishpond Wood, and at the junction go left to re-enter Bewerley. *Tucked secretively away on the right is Bewerley Grange Chapel, built as a grange by Marmaduke Huby, Abbot of Fountains from 1494-1526: his motto is inscribed on the outside wall. It was sympathetically restored in 1965, and stands in peaceful grounds a world apart from Pateley just over the river.* **Continue through the village to complete the walk by the opening steps back to Bridgehouse Gate and into Pateley Bridge.**

Bewerley Grange Chapel

MERRYFIELD MINES

START Pateley Bridge   Grid ref. SE 157655

DISTANCE 6½ miles

ORDNANCE SURVEY MAPS
1:50,000
Landranger 99 - Northallerton & Ripon
1:25,000
Explorer 26 - Nidderdale

ACCESS Town centre car parks; buses run from Harrogate.

A splendid all-weather excursion on well-defined tracks and paths.

☐ *From the foot of the High Street cross the bridge and turn immediately into the park on the right. Remaining on the wooded riverbank, a good path (initially surfaced) leads through the first caravan site of the day before gaining open fields. In the second field the path cuts the corner at Foster Beck's entry into the Nidd, to a stile to the right of the prominent Brigg House Farm. Alongside a cottage a small footbridge crosses the beck, now followed upstream to a gate before striking across to the next gate onto a junction of lanes at Corn Close.*

Turn left along the road down-dale to reach the Watermill Inn. *Its magnificent waterwheel is 35ft in diameter, an iron and wood structure that after years of neglect was restored with pride in 1990. Steps lead from the car park to a precariously perched millpond, with ducks and donkeys in evidence. The wheel once served this former flax mill that itself operated as a ropemakers into the 1960s: conversion to an inn saw a chequered existence. Having once been a locally renowned folk venue, it now takes full advantage of its spacious grounds and unique setting to draw a clientele that includes, quite naturally, many families.*

Continue a little further along the road to a sharp bend, and here turn up a farm drive all the way to Mosscarr Farm, ignoring an uphill fork en route. Continuing behind the barns - which cluster island-like in the centre of the field - *the track runs on to a cottage, just beyond which is a footbridge in a charming wooded dell. Head downstream a few yards before striking away up a splendid green walled way to a track above Ashfold Side Beck. Turn right, descend to a bridge to join a farm road by a small caravan site.*

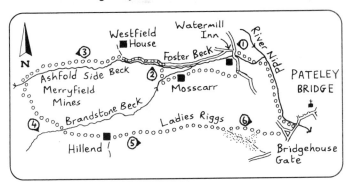

This strip of tarmac is followed left, clusters of caravans now appearing with regularity. At a steep fork to Westfield House Farm, remain on the level track into another site. Our track threads its way through to finally shrug off the last caravan just when it seemed we'd never be free of them. This same track - a typically well engineered mine road - leads all the way up this increasingly attractive side valley known as Merryfield Gill. Suddenly and dramatically old mine workings appear across the beck, and a footpath breaks off to drop to a gate beyond which a concrete ford crosses Ashfold Side Beck.

The Merryfield Mines provide a marvellous insight into the dale's important lead mining past, and the Prosperous Smelt Mill is one of the major sites. *The aim - allowing for any careful exploration - is to gain the far upper side of the workings. Behind the large ruinous building* which was the smelt mill - note the geared winding shaft forlornly in situ - is the prominent steep line of an old flue - at its foot *a narrow green path heads half-left through the heather to join a wide track. Turning right along it, the flue is again met below the remains of an old chimney. From here the track runs through the heart of the mines, at the foot of the main*

33

spoil-heaps. Alternatively, a more direct track slants from the ruin at a lower level to the other side. Approaching the wall at the far side turn left, and the track - at first a little sketchily - starts to climb above the site, passing one last ruin and levelling out before reaching a gate.

At the Merryfield Mines

Beyond it the track continues alongside a wall to arrive at Brandstone Dub Bridge, *a shapely structure with an attractive waterfall just below. The sides of this gill also supported a number of smelting mills.* **Cross it and head confidently away again, passing several farms as our way becomes a narrow surfaced lane.** *At a bend on crossing Coldstones Beck at Hillend,*

The Watermill Inn

the house up to the right was the Pateley Bridge youth hostel for the ten years up to 1956. *About five minutes beyond **Riggs House Farm** on lofty **Ladies' Rigg** - which offers outstanding views down dale to **Brimham Rocks** - the lane enters a shroud of trees. Here, and not before, leave it through the few trees on the left to a stile in a corner. Follow the hedge downhill with **Pateley Bridge** directly ahead, its High Street appearing near-vertical.*

*Keeping the field boundaries on the right, two gates are encountered before joining a back road at **Bridgehouse Gate**. Just in front is the former Metcalfe's brewery, converted to dwellings but retaining its typical small brewhouse appearance in a pleasing corner. From here the main road leads back over the bridge into town.*

Pateley Bridge

6

WATH & SCOT GATE

START Pateley Bridge   Grid ref. SE 157655

DISTANCE 4 miles

ORDNANCE SURVEY MAPS
1:50,000
Landranger 99 - Northallerton & Ripon
1:25,000
Explorer 26 - Nidderdale

ACCESS Town centre car parks; bus service from Harrogate.

Man's industrial influence on one small rural area could not be better portrayed than here, where on the edge of an old market town, forestry, quarrying, a light railway, an inclined tramway, a reservoir, and more distantly lead mining are observed.

☐ **From the bridge at the foot of the High Street, head up this main thoroughfare and turn left along Church Street. Past the church continue along Wath Road. After the last house on the left it crosses a bridge.** *This is the immediately evident course of the inclined tramway that once served the Scot Gate Ash Quarry high above.* **A stile gives access to the now grassy incline, whose steep, unswerving course leads unfailingly to the old workings.** *Pauses to savour the view back over the town are strongly recommended!*

In these surprisingly extensive workings 'delphstone' was won, the particular strength of this form of millstone grit seeing it used as platforms and steps of important public buildings and works. The tramway was built in 1873 by local entrepreneur George Metcalfe, and operated by steel ropes with the loaded trucks descending a maximum 1 in 3 gradient as they assisted the empty ones to return to the quarry. The descent of 600 feet over a distance of 1000 yards ended at the railway yard at the bottom, where it was transferred to a standard gauge railway for the next leg of its journey, out of the valley. It is very much within living memory that the quarry was still a major source of employment.

With the remains of the tramway terminal directly ahead, a track heads left, keeping close company with a fence and wall. This clear path crosses the lower boundary of the quarry's heathery environs to reach a gate. From a stile there, cross the field to a similar combination to emerge onto a narrow lane.

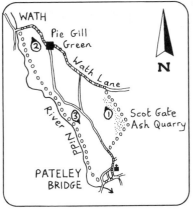

This quiet byway leads downhill, eventually back to the valley. *During this extended descent one can reap the rewards of the incline's steep pull and concentrate exclusively on the glorious* panorama, a major feature of which is the penetration of the upper dale by the finger-like Gouthwaite Reservoir. Nidderdale's vast moorlands form the horizons, while back down-dale the 'golf balls' of the Menwith Hill base intrude.

At a junction continue straight ahead, descending to another junction at the delightfully named Pie Gill Green and then right for just a couple of minutes into Wath. *This unspoilt little settlement boasts a charming wooded setting: it is a desperate shame that there are no rights of way by which to explore the hills and gills of its hinterland.* **Turn left along the road,** *passing the inn sporting a fine sign of great individuality.*

At Wath

37

Wath Bridge

*On the left, past the inn, the former station house confirms the presence of the old railway, now merely a grassy embankment which we shall soon join. **A little further, Wath Bridge crosses the Nidd to meet the valley road**, a lovely arched structure embowered in greenery, still small enough to recall the days when as a packhorse bridge it served the monks of Fountains Abbey. **Without crossing it, take a contrastingly simple footbridge on the left, from where a path crosses a field to a stile, continuing on to meet the unmistakable course of the old railway.***

38

The Nidd Valley Light Railway was opened in 1908 by Bradford Corporation to convey materials and men for the construction of Angram Reservoir. It also operated a passenger service for two decades, but the completion of the Scar House dam in 1936 brought an end to its useful life.

At Wath lane end

From the next stile the line is followed for some distance, to a point where the Nidd comes within a stone's throw. Beyond a stile in this tree-shrouded setting the railway is forsaken for the river, whose tree-lined bank leads unerringly back to Pateley Bridge. Partway along, the arrival of Foster Beck creates a lively confluence. **On reaching a weir the path becomes confined and is deflected away to emerge between buildings onto a short lane immediately adjacent to Pateley's graceful bridge.**

Looking over Pie Gill Green to Gouthwaite Reservoir

7

GOUTHWAITE RESERVOIR

START Wath   Grid ref. SE 144677

DISTANCE 7 miles

ORDNANCE SURVEY MAPS
1:50,000
Landranger 99 - Northallerton & Ripon
1:25,000
Explorer 26 - Nidderdale

ACCESS Start from the sizeable parking area by the bus stop at Wath Bridge. An alternative start is a more recently opened car park part-way along the shore of the reservoir (GR 126693). This has the advantage of breaking up the long road section - see note below. Summer Sunday buses from Pateley Bridge.

A complete circuit of Gouthwaite Reservoir, most 'natural' of Nidderdale's man-made lakes, and a birdwatcher's paradise: binoculars are a worthwhile addition to the rucksack's contents.

Before starting out it should be noted that due to Nidderdale's sometimes inadequate path network, one-third of this walk must follow the valley road, not an entirely satisfactory arrangement. It does, however, enjoy superb views over the reservoir. This is neither A or B road, nor a through route of any note, but it serves the communities of the upper dale and attracts more than an occasional vehicle. The first half could be undertaken as a linear walk, if transport arrangements can be resolved.

☐ Widened a century ago, Wath Bridge maintains its intimate character sufficient to recall the days when it served the monks of Fountains Abbey and the packhorse trade. **On crossing the bridge, take a stile to accompany the Nidd upstream. After a** *second stile the path crosses the centre of a field to enter trees:* the roar of water leaving Gouthwaite's hidden dam increases. **A stile and gate lead to a locked gate at the eastern end of the dam.** Constructed in 1901, this 80-foot high dam is well camouflaged by foliage, which sets the scene for the least intrusive of the Nidderdale reservoirs. A mostly naturally wooded shoreline masks the harshness of man's hand: indeed, it could be argued that this is merely a return to colder times, when a glacial lake filled the dale floor here. **The path takes a stile opposite to rise across two fields to join a broad track:** the geography of the walk can now be well appraised from this early vantage point.

Following the track left, it soon descends almost to the very shore of the reservoir. All that separates us is the green line of the old Nidd Valley Light Railway, completed by Bradford Corporation in 1908 to transport materials and men to construct the Angram dam at the dalehead. For a couple of decades passenger services also operated along this section to Lofthouse, though the line itself only survived as long as it was needed to serve construction of the second great dam at Scar House.

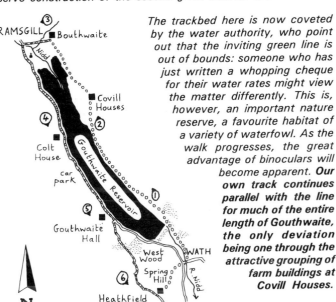

The trackbed here is now coveted by the water authority, who point out that the inviting green line is out of bounds: someone who has just written a whopping cheque for their water rates might view the matter differently. This is, however, an important nature reserve, a favourite habitat of a variety of waterfowl. As the walk progresses, the great advantage of binoculars will become apparent. **Our own track continues parallel with the line for much of the entire length of Gouthwaite, the only deviation being one through the attractive grouping of farm buildings at Covill Houses.**

41

Covill (Covell) Houses is an ancient settlement mentioned in Domesday, and at one time a grange of Fountains Abbey. From here there is a view of both Ramsgill and Middlesmoor villages. **The surfaced farm road leads out to reach Bouthwaite at the head of the reservoir.** *Ramsgill's smaller neighbour was a more important grange of Fountains.* **A left turn at this crossroads of lanes leads to Nidd Bridge on the edge of Ramsgill.** *Note first, however, a 'Pateley' clock on the barn wall oppposite, and en route a small Wesleyan chapel of 1890 and then the course of the railway, one last time, at the former station house.*

Ramsgill is a visually striking village on the banks of its own beck just short of its confluence with the Nidd. Prime feature is the

spacious green, where mellow cottages and flowery gardens play support to the imposing ivy clad hotel. Since extended, this former shooting lodge of the Yorke family still bears their name. In earlier times Ramsgill was a major grange of Byland Abbey, and at the rear of the church a solitary gable-end is all that now remains of the monks' chapel. The solid church was rebuilt in 1843, and looks out across the reedy head of the reservoir.

St Mary the Virgin,
Ramsgill

After a sojourn on the green, continue south on the road out of the village. Gouthwaite Reservoir soon returns, and the road clings to its shore for two winding miles to reach the striking frontage of the 'new' Gouthwaite Hall, a 1901 replacement - including some original stonework - for the former seat of the Yorke family that had to make way for the reservoir.

Gouthwaite Hall

A little further, a narrow, winding strip of tarmac leaves the road through a cattle-grid. Unsignposted and resembling a private drive, this traffic-free lane rises steeply, affording extensive views back over the reservoir and further up-dale. *Passing through the dense West Wood, the road levels out to arrive at the scattered group of dwellings at Heathfield.* This ancient settlement once had a fulling mill under the auspices of the monks of Byland Abbey, while the ubiquitous Yorke family smelted ore here from their lead mines.

As the lane slowly descends, opt for the drive down to the left to Spring Hill Farm. The diverted path skirts the right-hand exterior of the buildings and yard and winds round to a stile at the far end of the field. From it descend half-left through two large fields, then straight over two smaller ones to drop steeply to the road at Wath lane end. The inn, incidentally, is just along the road into the hamlet, in a leafy setting just past the old station house and sporting a fine individual sign (see WALK 6).

8

FOUNTAINS EARTH MOOR

START Ramsgill   Grid ref. SE 119709

DISTANCE 8¼ miles

ORDNANCE SURVEY MAPS
1:50,000
Landranger 99 - Northallerton & Ripon
1:25,000
Explorer 26 - Nidderdale

ACCESS Start from the village centre. Cars must be parked diplomatically, taking care not to impinge on the green or block access, also being aware of notices indicating the parts reserved for hotel patrons. Summer Sunday buses from Pateley Bridge.

This bracing moorland ramble is entirely free of navigational difficulties, tracing old trackways throughout its length.

Ramsgill is the showpiece village of the upper dale. Prime feature is the spacious green, where attractive cottages and flowery gardens play support to the imposing ivy-clad hotel. Since extended, this former shooting lodge of the Yorke family still bears their name. In earlier times Ramsgill was an important grange of Byland Abbey, and at the rear of the church a solitary gable-end is all that remains of the monks' chapel. The church was rebuilt in 1843, and looks out across the reedy head of the reservoir.

☐ *From the green take the valley road towards Lofthouse, but immediately after crossing Nidd Bridge opt for the narrow lane to Bouthwaite. En route, the course of the old Nidd Valley Light Railway is crossed, adjacent to the old station house. Passing a small Wesleyan chapel of 1890, a junction of tracks at the hamlet of Bouthwaite is reached.* Noting a locally manufactured clock set into a barn wall on the left, **go straight ahead to a gate, beyond which a stony track scales the hillside.** Suitable halts reveal retrospective views over much of the valley, including Gouthwaite Reservoir. Beyond Ramsgill the appealing side-valley of Ramsgill Beck tumbles from the moors - another of Nidderdale's forbidden places. Nearer to hand, just above Lul Beck, a small slate quarry operated into the early 20th century.

When the gradient eases the going underfoot improves, rising all the way to Intake Gate and a junction at a wall corner. Until recently a standard road-sign stood here, a curious feature on a clearly unmotorable road: it has since been replaced by an even more modern sign proclaiming the obvious, though reckless off-roaders having got this far have already done the hard bit: all in

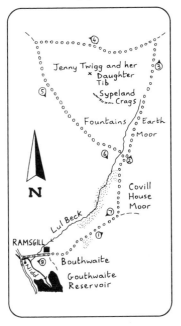

all, surely a daft place for such a sign! The track continuing uphill is the old road to Kirkby Malzeard via Dallowgill. **Branch left to a second fork, to which we shall later return.** Once important highways that linked upper Nidderdale with its monastic landlords today serve only walkers, shooting parties and the occasional off-road biker.

With a choice of gates, opt for the right fork, a modern shooters' way overlaying a historic track rising gently through the heather of Fountains Earth Moor. Across parallel Lul Beck the outcrops of Sypeland Crags break the near skyline. The moor is named from its early owners, for Fountains Abbey - less than 10 miles distant - had an important grange at Bouthwaite. It is interesting to note that while Nidderdale was in the grip of monastic landlords, it was shared by two abbeys that often had their differences: what they did agree on, by and large, was

45

access on certain routes across Fountains' land to enable Byland monks and workers to reach their possessions on the western side of the valley.

Looking back over Gouthwaite Reservoir from the track to the moor

Higher up the track, beyond a gate, an inscribed boundary stone is passed before reaching a T-junction. This is also marked by an old guidepost, the right branch being the old road that engages several more upland miles towards Kirkby Malzeard and Masham. **Go left to commence a level march.** By now the underestimated vastness of these great sweeping moors is fully appreciated: the great upland stretching east is criss-crossed by old trackways without a motor road in evidence save for the Lofthouse-Masham strip of tarmac, and even that is a relatively recent 'improvement'.

At a stone shooting house, halt at the gate to identify Jenny Twigg and her Daughter Tib, two rock towers on the near skyline. Sat high on the moor these natural obelisks are unfortunately on private land. **Resuming, another junction will be reached: here go left, inevitably, again on a superb green road for the most part enclosed by walls.** Less historic than its counterparts, this was made at the time of the enclosures. **In due course it leads back to the outward track, and all that remains is the wholly pleasurable task of retracing the opening two miles.**

9

THE HEART OF NIDDERDALE

START Ramsgill   Grid ref. SE 119709

DISTANCE 5 ½ miles

ORDNANCE SURVEY MAPS
1:50,000
Landranger 99 - Northallerton & Ripon
1:25,000
Explorer 26 - Nidderdale **or**
Outdoor Leisure 30 - Yorkshire Dales North/Central

ACCESS Start from the village centre. Park diplomatically, not impinging on the green or blocking access, and also being aware of notices indicating parts reserved for hotel patrons. Lofthouse has better parking. Summer Sunday buses from Pateley Bridge.

Lofthouse and Ramsgill are the two valley floor villages of upper Nidderdale: this walk links them by easy field paths each side of the river. For the effort involved the views are outstanding, though curiously there is little direct contact with the river itself.

Ramsgill is the showpiece village of the dale. Attractive cottages and flowery gardens line the spacious green, and play support to the imposing ivy clad hotel. Since extended, this former shooting lodge of the Yorke family still bears their name. In earlier times Ramsgill was an important grange of Byland Abbey, and at the rear of the church a solitary gable-end is all that remains of the monks' chapel. The solid looking church was rebuilt in 1843, and looks out across the reedy head of the reservoir.

☐ ***The path to Lofthouse leaves the upper, smaller green by way of a farmyard, and from a gate at the far end a good path heads off through the fields for West House Farm. After a gate by the*** *river a succession of stiles interrupt the uncomplicated start, and after passing a large barn the path climbs to West House. Skirting to the right of its confines the path heads directly away, ignoring the farm drive which heads down towards the road. Running a clear course through the fields,* the path now enjoys spacious views up-dale to Lofthouse, Middlesmoor and beyond: a superb panorama. *Becoming a little fainter the path bears slightly right along a grassy rake to a stile, continuing away to join another farm track. This leads down to a bridge on Blayshaw Gill and on to a T-junction of walled tracks. Turning right, the track descends to Studfold and swings left to join the cul-de-sac road to Stean.*

Turn right over a bridge and past the Middlesmoor junction to a lay-by: here take a kissing-gate, passing between barn and cricket pitch to a similar gate. Cross the water authority Scar House road and down to a foot-bridge over the Nidd (noting first that a path runs up the near bank to the charmingly hidden Nidd Falls), from where a path leads up to the right to enter a corner of Lofthouse.

The village is entered by the attractive stone water fountain, with the homely Post office just behind. Commence the return leg by going right a short way, then turning off between the memorial institute and the hotel car park. Just along it, a stile on the right leads to a diagonal field-crossing to another stile. Follow the wall right, crossing a further field before dropping to the road. Have a good look over the wall to locate Nidd Heads - here the true river returns to daylight at a rocky door, after a lengthy underground spell since the environs of Goyden Pot several miles further up-dale.

48

Nidd Heads

Turn left for five minutes on the road, then from a stile on the right head half-right to a stile beyond a barn. From a stile by a rusting barn the track-bed of the Nidd Valley Light Railway is joined: its grassy embankment leads quickly back onto the road. The old railway line was built to aid construction of the dale-head reservoirs, but was also exploited to operate a passenger service from Pateley Bridge up to Lofthouse. Unfortunately it was dismantled after serving its main function.

Nidd Falls,
Lofthouse

Cross straight over just as the railway did, and follow it a short way only to a stile, then slant up two fields before the slope eases, and heading away from it an enclosed path leads below a plantation to Longside House. Until 1983 this was a superbly sited youth hostel, but its demise underlines the 'unfashionable' face of Nidderdale. Currently it continues to welcome walkers, however, as a guest house. The views from this neighbourhood are truly magnificent, both up and down dale, and across to the moors above Ramsgill. **Passing between the trees and the rear of the house, the path runs on through a gate to Longside Farm.**

Again keeping round the back, a sketchy path contours across to a stile, and from there along successive field bottoms to a stile in front of the wooded environs of Lul Beck. This easy section enjoys views down the valley to the still waters of Gouthwaite Reservoir: also clearly discernible below is a substantial length of the old railway line through the fields. From it drop steeply to a gap-stile, then over a farm bridge into the hamlet of Bouthwaite.

The fountain at Lofthouse

Ramsgill's smaller neighbour enjoyed similar status in monastic times, when it was a grange of Fountains Abbey. **Go ahead to a junction of lanes, there turning right,** past the tiny Wesleyan chapel of 1890 and then the old station house, with the platform and footings of the railway bridge still evident. **The slim lane runs out to the junction at Nidd Bridge, here turning left to re-enter Ramsgill.**

The Yorke Arms and the green, Ramsgill

10

HOW STEAN GORGE

START Lofthouse   Grid ref. SE 101735

DISTANCE 4½ miles

ORDNANCE SURVEY MAPS
1:50,000
Landranger 99 - Northallerton & Ripon
1:25,000
Explorer 26 - Nidderdale **or**
Outdoor Leisure 30 - Yorkshire Dales North/Central

ACCESS Car park in the village, with additional parking at either How Stean Gorge approach, or Middlesmoor. Summer Sunday bus service from Pateley Bridge.

Any visit to How Stean Gorge is a trip to remember, but this excursion adds the natural attractions outwith the ravine. Though not a necessary requisite, a torch will be of assistance if contemplating any extra-curricular adventures, of which more shortly....

❏ *Leave the village by a track between cottages behind the water fountain, across from the Post office. A path descends to a footbridge over the Nidd, after which cross straight over the Scar House road to a kissing-gate. Pass between the cricket pitch and a barn to a similar gate in the wall-corner ahead: here the road is joined at a lay-by that offers yet another starting point. Turn right for a few yards, and then left on the fork to Stean.*

Before bridging How Stean Beck the gorge car park is passed, whilst immediately after it, take a farm road left to Studfold. If seeking a more direct route to the gorge, simply remain on the road. An outdoor centre and a caravan site share the farming environs. Avoid the farm by remaining on the track which swings right to climb steeply past cottages. Continue up past a branch left, and immediately after a barn-cum-derelict farmhouse take a gate on the right. A track of sorts heads along the field bottoms to Whitbeck Farm. En route enjoy super views over Lofthouse up to Thrope Edge and the moorland skyline, while Middlesmoor sits on its hill, and the valley of How Stean Beck, subject of our walk, is well revealed.

A slim stile to the right accesses the drive, then go left up into the yard. Turn immediately right to drop to a footbridge, then resume along the field bottoms to approach the next farmhouse. Cross its drive left of the barn ahead, and on through gap-stiles to approach Stean. Dropping down, a slab bridge crosses a tiny beck and enters an attractive corner of Stean. Like Studfold earlier, here was a small grange of Byland Abbey. The immediate visitor attractions of this farming hamlet consist of a phone box, but its famous gorge makes it a Yorkshire favourite.

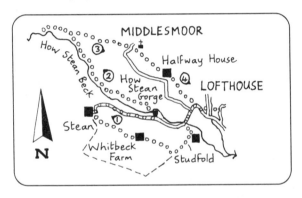

Turn downhill to leave by the access road, soon passing, at a bend, a stile sending a path down to a footbridge over How Stean Beck - a useful short cut if not visiting the gorge. Otherwise the road runs quickly along to the entrance to How Stean Gorge, passing How Stean Tunnel on the right. An entrance fee is payable at the cafe, where full meals can be obtained. It also has a small gift shop, toilets, and peacocks patrolling the grounds. How Stean Gorge is a marvellous natural spectacle, a limestone ravine half a mile long and up to 80 feet deep. The rocks have been worn into dramatic contours by the action of the swift-flowing water, and deep, dark and wet caves abound.

The entire expedition is but a short one, the part downstream of the cafe being especially exciting as the path crosses dramatically suspended bridges to guarded natural walkways through the rocks. Of greatest interest, perhaps, are How Stean Tunnel, near the walk's upper limit, and the cave known as Tom Taylor's Chamber. Legend says it acquired its name from an outlaw who sought refuge here, but what is more certain is that Roman coins were unearthed in the 19th century. This 530ft cave runs from the gorge out into the field behind the cafe, and even novice troglodytes might negotiate it with the aid of a torch (which can be hired from the cafe).

How Stean Gorge

On emerging, resume the walk by crossing the bridge to the car park field and locate a gate at the top left corner. Advance to a gate left of a barn, then go left across fields to meet a path descending from Middlesmoor at a fine wall-stile. Turn down the field to approach a footbridge, and here (without crossing it) continue upstream, now hugging the spritely beck. This section proves there is much more to How Stean Beck than its obvious attraction: below Stean, rock walls already confine it, whilst upstream a smaller waterfall - difficult to see from the path - precedes the highlight, the Aysgarth-like How Stean Force. **Initially thin, the path runs on above an old kiln,** *still in suffcient repair to form a suitable temporary shelter under a rocky shelf.* **Entering woodland, the path soon rises up to the top corner. While the route doubles back here, first descend into the large pasture, with How Stean Force visible just ahead. The best viewpoint involves crossing a bridge over an inflowing tributary to draw level with the falls.**

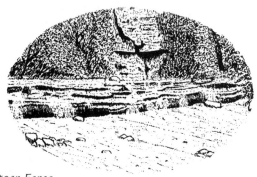

How Stean Force

From the waterfall retrace steps to the stile on the edge of the wood, where a second stile is located just a few yards up to the left. From it climb through bracken to a gateway, then bear half-right to a stile in a fence. *This is a fine vantage point for the remote qualities of the How Stean valley.* **Follow a hedge away to another stile, then slant across a large field up to a gate.** *By now the view has extended down the dale to bring in the tranquil waters of Gouthwaite Reservoir.* **From here a track runs to the farm ahead, but the path has been diverted along a pleasanter green track rising to the far corner. A wooded enclosure behind the farm leads down to emerge onto the road at the entrance to Middlesmoor, opposite the old Wesleyan chapel of 1899.**

Middlesmoor is Nidderdale's first village, sharing its allegiance to the main dale with the major tributary that is the subject of this walk. Its name accurately describes this position, on a broad tongue between the two valleys. Just above is a particularly attractive corner where the inn and the Post office stand.

Leave the village by making for the church, reached by any of several winding byways between hoary stone cottages. St Chads was rebuilt in 1866, and a 7th century Saxon cross inside is said to be Chad's preaching cross. The churchyard is renowned for its view down the valley, one that can be savoured during the impending steady return to the dale floor. To its right is a stile, and a short snicket descends to a gate. A long flight of steps leads down into a field, from where a path maintains a straight line to Halfway House Farm. Go straight through the yard to a gate at the end, and head down the right side of a field to a stile. In the next but one field cross to a stile in the far left, to emerge back onto the lay-by near the start of the walk. Retrace steps back over the footbridge, but first consider a five-minute detour upstream to enjoy the shy charms of Nidd Falls.

St Chads,
Middlesmoor

GOYDEN POT

START Lofthouse   Grid ref. SE 101735

DISTANCE 7 miles

ORDNANCE SURVEY MAPS
1:50,000
Landranger 99 - Northallerton & Ripon
1:25,000
Explorer 26 - Nidderdale **or**
Outdoor Leisure 30 - Yorkshire Dales North/Central

ACCESS Start from the car park in the village centre. Summer Sunday bus service from Pateley Bridge.

Lofthouse is a small, tidy village high above the river, focal point being the attractive corner which includes the homely Post office and an attractive water fountain which bears words worth reading. Further down are the village hall, Crown Hotel, and school, which serves all of the upper dale's youngsters. The former station was the highest on the Nidd Valley Light Railway (of which more later), which carried passengers from Pateley Bridge and the outside world.

☐ *Leave the village by the Masham road. Only car exit from the upper dale, it was only made fit for motors in the 1960s. **The houses cling to this road until shrugged off to begin its immediate climb. Before the first bend, however, leave by a level track to the left. This is Thrope Lane, and beyond a gate it undulates above the Nidd to lead unerringly to Thrope Farm.** Once a small grange of Fountains Abbey, Thrope had its own watermill until a century ago.*

Remain on the track past the farm, to gradually drop to the stony course of the river, or more likely its dry bed. Continue upstream a short distance to Dry Wath, a suitable name for the ford we use to cross to a gate. A good path continues beyond it, soon re-entering the wooded confines of the curving river bed. When a stile returns this old way to the fields, it rises to join the drive to Limley Farm. This attractive grouping is on the site of another grange, this time of Byland Abbey.

Head through the yard, turning first right and then left to pass round the buildings. Behind the last barn a path descends through a nettle-field to cross the river bed to a gate. Beyond it carry on by a collapsed wall, past a barn to join a track which zigzags up the steep wooded bank. At the top it leads to a gate to enter the confines of Thwaite House, where refreshments might be available. Originally a grange of Fountains Abbey, this was, until a few years ago, falling into decay. From a gateway to the left of the buildings head off along an enclosed track, soon emerging into more open country to contour a great loop around to the farm of Bracken Ridge. This section boasts particularly spacious views of the upper dale.

Behind the farm gate, turn right up the drive which swings left to begin a long traverse of The Edge. Not to be confused with the higher level Dale Edge (see WALK 12), this wide track is a splendid platform along which several farms and cottages are based. At several locations in the vicinity, coal was mined as far back as monastic times. With a wall to the left and steep slopes to the right, it runs on pleasurably until, beyond the last farm, New Houses Edge Farm, the track fords a beck and enters a field: just a little further take a track which branches left to descend. On reaching a gate near a barn the track crosses fields to approach the river, which it follows downstream to New Houses Bridge.

New Houses
Edge Farm
The Edge
Edge
Farm ④ ③
Bracken
Ridge
Nidd
New
Houses
Thwaite
House
⑤
Goyden
Pot
Limley
Farm
Thrope
Farm
⑥ ①
N
Thrope Lane
LOFTHOUSE

*Do not cross the shapely structure but head along the track into
New Houses Farm, whose predecessor was a dairy farm under
the auspices of Fountains Abbey. Turn right after the first
building to a small gate. A few yards beyond is a large gate: from
it head away with the wall to a stile near the river. Follow the Nidd
downstream, trading banks at a footbridge. After a pair of nearby
stiles the swallow-hole of Manchester Hole is reached under the
cliff of Beggarmoat Scar, and the Nidd quietly departs underground. Note, up on the road, a bricked up former railway tunnel.
Only five minutes further downsteam - or down-bed - is the dark
hole of Goyden Pot itself.*

Goyden Pot

When the flow of water is
sufficiently strong, the ex-
cess from Manchester Hole
is carried a further 300 yards
down to this point. It then
enjoys a subterranean course
for two miles, re-emerging
below Lofthouse at Nidd
Heads (see WALK 9). While
the main chamber of Goyden
Pot can easily be entered, the
inner depths contain a maze
of passages best left to the
well-equipped, many of whom frequent this locale in rubber suits
and minibuses. If confused by the sound of running water in this
largely dry environment, turn for an answer to nearby Limley Gill.

*From Goyden Pot continue down the grassy bank, soon crossing
Limley Gill and quickly becoming enclosed to return to Limley
Farm: before entering the yard, note the intriguing dry 'river'*

Thwaite
House

58

bend here - quite unreal. **Bear right out of the yard, from where one can either trace outward steps through Dry Wath to Thrope Farm, or join the water authority road. By turning left this will return to the toll-booth at its beginning, near Lofthouse.**

Not just our playground: near Thrope Farm in late summer 1985

At the drive to Thrope Farm, however, there is a chance to rejoin the riverbank for a few field's-lengths: a hurdle stile on the west bank of the river admits to the grassy bank that leads pleasurably through several stiles. The tree-lined Nidd, with its sometimes slabby rock bed is a pleasure to follow, until forced up onto the road on arrival at a blocked, pathless wood. *Whilst maps suggest a public path all the way, it is largely impassable.* **With its broad verges, the road is dead level.** *This last feature is due to this being the course of the Nidd Valley Light Railway, constructed by Bradford Corporation in 1908 to facilitate the transport of men and materials for building the Angram dam at the dale-head. It was dismantled after similar work on the Scar House dam, and so this road came into use on the back of the railway's hard work.*

At the tollbooth turn left to a footbridge over the river, but before crossing, a short detour upstream leads through a stile in a low wall to locate the charming Nidd Falls in a dark, wooded dell. On returning to cross the bridge, a path to the right leads up into the centre of Lofthouse.

DALE EDGE

START Middlesmoor   Grid ref. SE 092742

DISTANCE 9 miles

ORDNANCE SURVEY MAPS
1:50,000
Landranger 99 - Northallerton & Ripon
1:25,000
Explorer 26 - Nidderdale **or**
Outdoor Leisure 30 - Yorkshire Dales North/Central

ACCESS Car park at the top of the village, past the last houses.

Middlesmoor is the first village in Nidderdale and probably the most interesting: built on neither the Nidd nor a tributary, it stands, as its name implies, on the vast tongue of moorland between the How Stean valley and that of the upper Nidd. At a windswept near-thousand feet up, the residents are clearly a hardy breed! The Crown Hotel retains a community need in this tiny settlement.

☐ **Leave the car park and turn right up In Moor Lane, which immediately downgrades into a rough track. This wide, stony way leads unceasingly but gradually upwards.** *After about half a mile look out for an inscribed standing stone on the left. This route is the old road from Middlesmoor to Coverdale, by way of the Lodge (see WALK 14): its approach to the Lodge was drowned by the construction of the reservoir, and its purpose further diminished by construction of the road to the dams on the bed of the old railway.* **Eventually the way levels out on the moor-top. Beyond a gate it finally runs free, and quickly starts a steeper descent towards Scar House Reservoir.** *Ahead now, in a great sweep is the majestically wild upper reach of Nidderdale, with Great and Little Whernsides encircling the reservoirs. Directly opposite are the extensive former Carle Side Quarries.*

Descend to the water authority road on the shore of Scar House Reservoir. Turn right as far as the dam, then cross it. Continue on the track past the rest-house, then take the branch right, rising to a gate. A little beyond, marshy ground is encountered, but the path soon picks up to continue to another gate before dropping to cross Woo Gill and a tributary in quick succession.

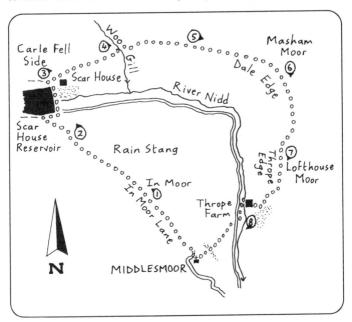

Shortly after vacating their deep confines, forsake the wide track for a lesser path climbing to a prominent little spoil heap on the left. Here also is an old mine shaft, around which great caution should be exercised, for water dropping down this shaft confirms its substantial depth. While Nidderdale is better known for its history of lead mining, coal was also mined here as far back as monastic times. From this vantage point one has the rare opportunity to appraise all three of Nidderdale's reservoirs. A good path again heads away to the right, quickly crossing the ugly scar of a new, bulldozed shooters' track, and commencing a near level trek around Dale Edge, remaining around 1400ft for a good two miles.

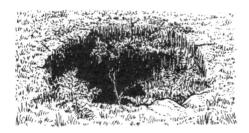

An old mineshaft
by the track to
Dale Edge

With magnificent views and a grand path the whole way, instructions are superfluous as you contour round the large loop of the valley. Long strides are the order of the day as the views along the length of the dale rank superlatives: a fine contrast is formed by the green of the valley at our feet and the dark outlines of rounded Meugher and the two Whernsides on the western skyline.

At a crossroads of green ways the other track drops back down to the farms on The Edge, and its left branch crosses over towards Masham (see WALK 15). Just through the gate an inscribed stone has long since weathered into illegibility. **Eventually the way arrives at the unmistakable shooting house on Thrope Edge.** From the valley road far below this appears as a church silhouetted on the skyline.

The shooting house
on Thrope Edge

Just before reaching the shooting house a path zigzags down to a gate then heads a little more gently left before swinging sharp right on reaching a wood. From the gate at the bottom **follow a fence left to a gate in it. Descend to a barn and onto the track behind Thrope Farm,** site of a small grange of Fountains Abbey. **Turn right and then sharp left into the yard, going right of the farm to the drive, down to the river.**

On crossing the Nidd, take a hurdle stile to head off down the grassy bank. Halfway through the second field, bear right to a mid-way gate in the wall, and continue across to a stile near the top corner. Cross straight over the water authority road to another stile, and slant diagonally up several fields with stiles prominent. Through a pencil wood aim across a large field, locating two further stiles and then a gate to re-enter Middlesmoor near the church.

Middlesmoor's attractive church was rebuilt in 1866 on an ancient foundation: a Saxon cross within is said to have been the 7th century preaching cross of St. Chad. It is better known, perhaps, as a viewpoint, the churchyard providing a foreground to a renowned panorama down the length of the dale, to Gouthwaite Reservoir and beyond. Re-entering the tiny village, one is immediately aware of the intricate network of alleyways that interlace between gritstone cottages.

On the descent to Scar House Reservoir from Rain Stang, looking across the dam to Carle Side and the extensive quarry remains

```
┌─────────────────────────────────────────┐
│              ⟨ 13 ⟩                       │
│                                           │
│      NIDD HEAD RESERVOIRS                 │
│                                           │
└─────────────────────────────────────────┘
```

START Scar House   Grid ref. SE 068766

DISTANCE 4½ miles

ORDNANCE SURVEY MAPS
1:50,000
Landranger 98 - Wensleydale & Upper Wharfedale
            99 - Northallerton & Ripon
1:25,000
Explorer 26 - Nidderdale (tiny section omitted) **or**
Outdoor Leisure 30 - Yorkshire Dales North/Central

ACCESS Just beyond Lofthouse, on the Middlesmoor road, a private water company road turns off to run the final miles to the dalehead. Subject to various restrictions this is open to the public, with a toll payable at the entrance. The main restrictions are a limit on the number of vehicles, and closure of the road at the end of the day. At the roadhead is a large car park with picnic area and toilets.

An extremely easy level circuit of Scar House Reservoir, which with its partner Angram Reservoir fills the head of Nidderdale.

☐ **From the car park join the water company road which runs past the dam of Scar House Reservoir. It is not crossed until the end of the walk. The road, meanwhile, runs along the entire length of the reservoir's southern shore.** *At the dale head, Great Whernside's rippling shoulders form a comprehensive barrier, making it difficult to imagine that such a cosy village as Kettlewell could be only a couple of miles down its other flank. Over to the right is the flat-topped Little Whernside.* **The road eventually gains the foot of Angram Reservoir by way of a rest house.** *This quaint facility is provided by the water company, and is certainly appreciated if caught by a sudden shower.*

64

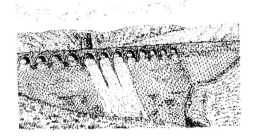

Angram Dam

Identical in character (though Scar House is double the size) Angram was completed in 1913, 23 years before its lower neighbour. Both the handiwork of Bradford Corporation, each boasts a masonry dam of which Scar House's rises to a height of no less than 150 feet. Beneath Angram's waters is a farm that was once the highest in the dale, on the site of a small grange of Byland Abbey.

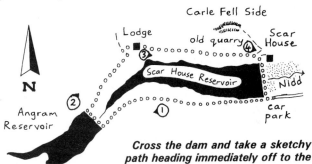

Cross the dam and take a sketchy path heading immediately off to the right from an old kissing-gate. After a slight descent, the path makes its level way past long-collapsed walls to a gate by Wench Gill, then up slightly to a gate in a wall. A little further and another wall-corner is reached. The path runs alongside to cross a stile in an intervening fence, and a gate admits to the terminus of a green lane. The enclosed track rises then swings sharp right to the unmistakable cluster of trees around the Lodge. The scant ruins are all that remains of what was once a medieval hunting lodge, and a working farm until within a century ago. Embowered in trees, this location is prominent in all views around this otherwise bleak dalehead.

65

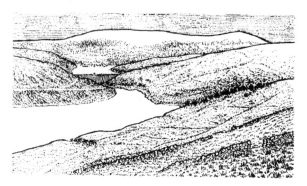

Scar House and Angram from Carle Fell Side, Great Whernside beyond

This same track now leads high above Scar House Reservoir's northern shore, *enjoying views beyond the dam to a magnificent sweep of upper valley beneath the moors of Dale Edge. Across the valley, below the car park, is the site of the temporary village that existed during the construction years: here was a complete settlement, with little short of 100 children schooled here in the 1920s. On the hillsides, meanwhile, are the sites of quarries opened specifically to win stone for the dams. Everything was on site, including, no doubt, very soon the water!* **A second rest house is reached above the dam, with Scar House itself just ahead. Now cross the dam to return to the car park,** *and take a look back across the dam wall to the extensive Carle Side Quarry.*

Scar House Reservoir and Great Whernside from the rest house

14

LITTLE WHERNSIDE

START Scar House   Grid ref. SE 068766

DISTANCE 7¼ miles

ORDNANCE SURVEY MAPS
1:50,000
Landranger 98 - Wensleydale & Upper Wharfedale
                99 - Northallerton & Ripon
1:25,000
Outdoor Leisure 30 - Yorkshire Dales North/Central

ACCESS Just beyond Lofthouse on the Middlesmoor road, a private water company road turns off to run the final miles to the dalehead. Subject to various restrictions this is open to the public, with a toll payable at the entrance. The main restrictions are a limit on the number of vehicles, and closure of the road at the end of the day. At the roadhead is a car park with picnic area and toilets. Most of the walk is on permissive paths.

☐ *From the car park join the road along to Scar House Reservoir, and turn across the dam.* At once the objective is in clear view, to the right and in front of the mass of Great Whernside. *At the far end, leave the road at once and turn left along the shore. Initially unclear and a little damp, the path soon improves to travel most of the north shore.* Our path traces the course of a long-dismantled tramway used in the construction of the Angram dam. *After a tree-girt beck flowing down from the Lodge, a water company 'rest house' is reached.* This is one of three around Scar House, a quaint arrangement worthy of patronage. *Abandon the shore at a stile just beyond, and climb alongside a wall.*

The way becomes enclosed by walls and continues to a junction: just to the right, embowered in trees, is the site of the Lodge, and ahead is the return route. For now, however, ignore both and turn

67

through the gate on the left. A track heads off through rough pasture, with Little Whernside looming larger and much closer. Encountering one or two damp sections, the path rises through two more gateways. Beyond the second one the climbing is delayed by a long, near-level march on a slender but generally clear path. If it is lost, simply remain on the same contour to a gate in a sturdy wall climbing the fellside.

Through it turn right to climb the relatively steep Hard Bank, here briefly enjoying the real feel of a mountain ascent - dominated all the time by its bulky neighbour Great Whernside across to the left. *Eventually the going eases to follow what is by now a fence through tall peat groughs to a junction of fences on the summit ridge.*

Cross the stile there and follow the fence to the right. The cairn is found on the north side. A visit will entail the only incursion into the Yorkshire Dales National Park to be found in the entire book, and for that reason alone may be deemed worthwhile. Having experienced the glories of upper Nidderdale, it also proves the farcical nature of National Park boundaries. Easily located as the only cairn on the felltop, the summit could equally be claimed by any of a hundred other peat castles, some appearing distinctly higher than the chosen spot. If only the graceful rise of Little Whernside could have been sustained a further 300 or so feet, instead of this abrupt demise on a boggy plateau.

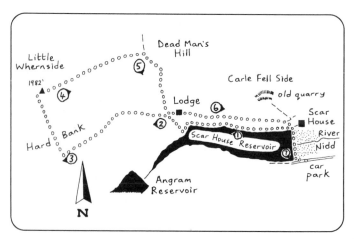

From the cairn the four major tops of the south-eastern dales are visible (see illustration). Further highlights include the rolling hills above Wensleydale and points north, while closer to hand shapely Penhill rises above the verdant green floor of Coverdale. Note the intricate patchwork of fields behind the farmstead of Woodale, almost at our feet at the head of Coverdale.

Back alongside the fence continue eastward through peat castles which at times block out all views. After a short, pronounced descent, with superb views down the length of Coverdale, **a longer, wetter stretch follows until a gate in the fence signals our meeting with the more solid Coverdale track.** This old packhorse road links the Coverdale villages with those of Nidderdale. From this, its crest, one can see ahead a shooting box on Dead Man's Hill, named after the discovery, 250 years ago, of the headless bodies of three Scottish pedlars buried in the peat. **Turn right along the old road, abandoning the watershed to drop down rapidly to the junction of tracks near the Lodge. Turn left to it,** passing between the low ruins that occupy the site of a medieval hunting lodge: within the last century it still functioned as a farm, and now it provides almost the only foliage of the walk. **Remain on this excellent track back to the foot of the reservoir.**

A second rest house is encountered a little too late to be of value, before re-crossing the dam. Look beyond the car park to locate the site of the temporary village that existed during the reservoir construction years: here was a complete settlement, with little short of 100 children schooled here in the 1920s. On the hillsides, meanwhile, are the sites of quarries opened specifically to win stone for the dams.

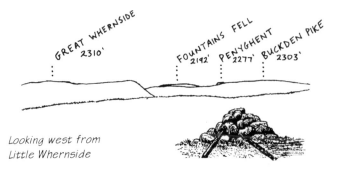

GREAT WHERNSIDE 2310' FOUNTAINS FELL 2192' PENYGHENT 2277' BUCKDEN PIKE 2303'

*Looking west from
Little Whernside*

69

15

COLSTERDALE

START Gollinglith Foot   Grid ref. SE 153809

DISTANCE 12 miles

ORDNANCE SURVEY MAPS
1:50,000
Landranger 99 - Northallerton & Ripon
1:25,000
Outdoor Leisure 30 - Yorkshire Dales North/Central
Pathfinder 630 - Middleham & Jervaulx Abbey

ACCESS Start from a parking area by the phone box, ensuring no local access is obstructed.

This bracing ramble is a substantial leg-stretcher, penetrating Colsterdale, valley of the river Burn, but also giving a promenade around the finest reach of Upper Nidderdale and concluding with an even less frequented side valley.

☐ **Unless the river Burn is very low, eschew the ford in favour of a footbridge from the corner of the parking area. From it turn upstream, past an attractively located house to rejoin the road from the ford: this at once becomes a track, on through a gate to run past an equine orientated establishment. Ignore both the turn into the farm, and a further branch left (our return route) and advance to a gate in front to begin a long march along the Coal Road.** *The Coal Road runs a magnificent route along the south side of Colsterdale, a gem of an old way largely untarnished by modern-day use: truly a classic.*

Colsterdale was exploited for coal by the monks of Jervaulx Abbey in lower Wensleydale, having been granted mining rights by the influental landowners the Scropes in 1334, and was still being mined until much more recent times. The Coal Road lives up to its name by providing access to long defunct pits that abound in the upper reaches of the Burn. Glorious panoramas reveal much of the Colsterdale scene. During these early stages enjoy the especially rich colour of Birk Gill Wood in the side valley opposite. Above, and more prominent, are Slipstone Crags fronting Agra Moor and the bracken clad moorland of Long Side.

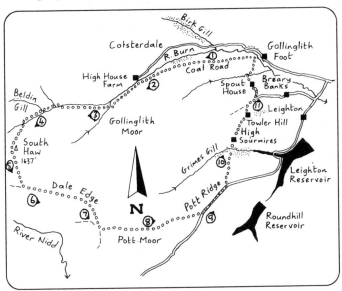

The track levels out at a prominent grassed-over pit, becoming even more exquisite as the immediate surrounds turn as colourful as the valley scenes. *Heather soon replaces bracken and the entire scene takes on a wilder mantle as the dalehead appears. Below, bracken reclaims the beckside, while above, sunken ways descend from abandoned coal or peat pits.* **Eventually the last farm in the valley (aptly named High House, on the opposite bank) appears and the track drops towards it: a stone bridge arches the Burn,** *here at last seen in the flesh. For a much shorter circuit, cross the bridge to the farm and return along the road.*

Resuming upstream, regain the main track by a green way above the beck, passing through a gate warning of old mine workings. *This is not the similarly inviting path - a bridleway on the map - by the beck.* **The track advances steadily up the valley side,**

crossing Thorny Grane Gill to reach a crossroads at a suburban looking shooters' house dated 1898. Near here in 1709 colliers cut through veins of lead, and though exploited, the modest amounts never approached the value of the coal deposits. Swinton estate signs confirm that we neither drop to the beck nor climb steeply by the side of the house, but continue on the obvious track parallel with the beck. A fine prospect down-dale identifies a very distant Slipstone Crags.

Forging into the final recesses of the dale, the track eventually drops to a low walled ruin near the beck, just beyond which is a fenced shaft. Yes, that track raking up the tongue ahead for the last mile or more is indeed ours. Our current track fords the beck then swings left up that tongue, from where further scars of new bulldozed tracks are revealed on the opposite bank.

The river Burn, above High House Farm

Today, tracks with centuries of history behind them are transformed into modern landrover tracks almost overnight: on more and more grouse shooting estates there seems an inability to reach the butts other than by motorised transport.

Rising up the spur the gradient eases to approach the modest ravine of Beldin Gill. Beyond it we're up in the wilds, as the worst of the new track suddenly ends. *Just above, a cairn is visible, and proves to be one of a pair made from a stone rectangle of uncertain origin.* **By now our objective, South Haw is prominent, silhouetted on the horizon ahead with its boundary stone atop the distinctive knoll. As the path fades, cling to a thin trod if possible, otherwise just aim for the knoll. Gentle slopes lead through peaty channels and heather, a green path further left may be found leading to a gate in the boundary fence at the right-hand base of South Haw.** *Through it, one is tempted up the grassy slope to the stone, a grand place to be.*

South Haw's boundary stone is inscribed 'Danby Mashamshire' and 'Netherdale Forest' - the old name for Nidderdale, which is now spread in front, though Great Whernside's mass and Little Whernside's flat top are only just visible over Carle Fell. Buckden Pike above Wharfedale enters the frame to the right of Little Whernside.

On South Haw

Back at the gate a distinct green path sets off through heather, contouring below the rounded top and then heading away. *First glimpse of water is Angram Reservoir at the dale-head.* **Though generally clear, this sometimes slender trod can become less so where heather has been burnt. If struggling, bear left as the descent becomes pronounced: one shouldn't go far wrong as the Dale Edge track cannot be overshot.** *After a keener descent,*

approaching a sheepfold, Scar House Reservoir appears, and our waiting track can already be traced for some distance. Drop between the fold and a shaft (solid stone construction, and very deep) to gain the smashing green way at a small cairn.

The head of Nidderdale in winter raiment, from Dale Edge. Great Whernside and Little Whernside form the backdrop, with Scar House Reservoir prominent. The walkers are returning down the track to The Edge (see WALK 11), from the crossroads where we depart the valley for Pott Moor.

Turn left to embark on a well-earned stroll for at least 1½ glorious miles, *enjoying superlative vistas throughout,* **to eventual arrival at a crossroads at a gate. Through it turn left on a superior green way past an illegibly weathered guidestone, bidding farewell to Nidderdale and within a minute crossing the brow** to be greeted by the return of the Cleveland Hills across the Vale of Mowbray. **Quickly reaching a gate, a fine shooters' track engages the heather of Pott Moor, dropping gently to join the Lofthouse-Masham road at an old milestone** - ahead is the Ilton Moor skyline.

Though not always very obvious, our return route henceforth traces a monastic trading route linking Lofthouse in upper Nidderdale with Jervaulx Abbey, continuing beyond Gollingith Foot by way of Ellingstring.

Go left a few minutes between moor and wall on a pleasant verge along Pott Ridge. Approaching a cattle-grid go left on a farm drive. Leaving a shooters' track going up the wall-side, advance through a gate labelled 'Grimes Gill House'. Leave the faint track at once by bearing right, down to a gate in a wall corner. Ahead is a nice prospect of this unfrequented side valley of Grimes Gill.

On the opposite slope is our next goal, the derelict farm of High Sourmire. Descend wall-side to the next gate, then a stile into dense bracken: a thin trod descends towards a few gnarled trees. Bearing a little right, cross a streamlet and down through a gateway in a wall bend. Down again, locate a tiny footbridge over the tinkling beck. Behind an oak the path spirals up the bank, quickly and steeply out of the bracken this time to a stile in the wall above. Rise by the wall-side to farm buildings, looking back over the valley and unknown terrain very typical of this area.

Go through a gateway between the buildings, but after the long barn on the left turn up to a gap-stile. Continue to the next stile above, with glimpses of Leighton Reservoir down to the right. *From it bear right, through the top end of a row of hawthorns to a sturdy stile in the wall above. Through a gateway in the fence behind, then follow the right-hand wall away to a stile in a gentle kink.* On the brow here is a view ahead to Slipstone Crags and Agra Moor. *Cross diagonally to Towler Hill Farm, and take a gate to its left to join its drive which runs out to a lane-head. Turn right down here,* admiring the prospect of Colsterdale country in front.

Reaching a junction, branch left down a road through the field to Spout House Farm, where the surface ends. Keep on through the yard on an enclosed way that drops to cross Spruce Gill Beck, then over a minor brow to return to the Coal Road. Go right to retrace the opening steps.

The old milestone
on Pott Ridge

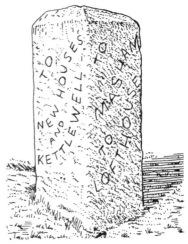

16

ILTON MOOR

START Ilton Druids' Temple   Grid ref. SE 177787

DISTANCE 9 miles

ORDNANCE SURVEY MAPS
1:50,000
Landranger 99 - Northallerton & Ripon
1:25,000
Explorer 26 - Nidderdale

ACCESS Start from the car park for the Druids' Temple, at the head of a cul-de-sac road off the minor road between Ilton and Healey, west of Masham. An alternative start is a lay-by just west of the anglers' car park at Leighton Reservoir.

☐ *Assuming the Druids' Temple is to be saved for the finish, return down the access road, and just as it becomes better surfaced where a farm drive comes in on the right, take a hurdle in the fence on the left, and cross the field with a line of telegraph poles bound for an obvious gap in the plantations.* The elaborate gateposts here suggest redundant stones from the temple. Low Knowle Farm is below in an attractive landscape, with plantations backed by high moorland - and the Cleveland Hills far across to the right. *Through the gate go left outside the plantation to a similar break half-way down. A track comes up from the farm, and once through, turn down the field-side with the green track winding down to a stile by a gate.* This superb grassy rake enjoys extensive views over the Leighton district to distant moors.

From the stile head diagonally down the field to a step-stile in the far corner above a small group of trees. Note the old boundary dyke at this corner. *Continue across to drop onto another seldom used green track. This soon enters scattered woodland and zigzags down the bank to Pott Beck.* Amid delightful surround-

ings turn upstream to a stone arched bridge. The track climbs a wall-side to run along right to a gate at the top. Curve round to the right up the field to a farm bridge above a barn, then incline steadily across the next field. Though the track swings up to a gate by farm buildings, continue on to a gate at the far top corner. Through it turn immediately left to rise up a short-lived way to the entrance to Leighton Hall Farm, here gaining the road through the hamlet. Dating from the 17th century, there had also been a chapel of ease here supplied by the monks of Fountains from their nearby Pott Grange.

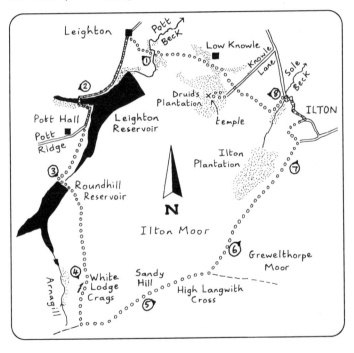

Go left along the Masham-Lofthouse road, passing reservoir office drives and then along the shore of Leighton Reservoir. Across the water rise the purple moors that will soon be underfoot. An anglers' car park and the alternative start lay-by are passed before the road bridges a finger of the upper reservoir then continues along the shore. As it swings away up Pott Bank,

bear left on a surfaced access road. This crosses the fields to Roundhill House, then runs along the top of the masonry dam of Roundhill Reservoir, commenced 1903, completed 1911.

Immediately across, vacate the main track and opt for the left-hand gate. A thin track rises straight up the rough pasture to a track reaching another gate. Enter the pasture, but again immediately vacate the track in order to climb the field to a gate in the top wall, giving access to the open moor. Here a distinct track slants up to the right, initially grooved. It affords a superb prospect over Roundhill Reservoir to the moorland bounding upper Nidderdale, and also reveals Leighton Reservoir, a long way back now. After the initial rise the way becomes a little less clear, running a generally level course parallel with the side-valley of Arnagill down to the right. Running past an assortment of gritstone boulders, largely on the left, the way remains sufficiently distinct to reach the modest outcrops of White Lodge Crags on the right (note the lone rowan) just after crossing a stream. This grand setting is a good place to devour lunch, and a pre-eminent vantage point. Looking back, a moorland tower in the near distance is a prominent landmark throughout the valley of Pott Beck.

Across Arnagill to Pott Ridge, from White Lodge Crags

Resuming, the way crosses a marshy gill - note, as before, the stone slab bridge evidencing this as a route once of some stature - *then rises to quickly join a broad track.* Visible well in advance as it rolls down from the higher moor to the right, this inter-valley route dates from monastic times, connecting upper Nidderdale with the Masham/Kirkby Malzeard district. Packhorses would be busy bringing lead and wool from the Nidderdale estates for onward carriage to the abbeys at Fountains and Byland. *Turn left in the foot - and hoof - steps of history, and let the rolling heather acres take over.*

Roundhill Reservoir from above Arnagill

Over the brow of Sandy Hill - at 1168ft the summit of the walk - *the way rolls on.* Look back over the moors across the now unseen reservoirs, to Great and Little Whernsides and farther right to Penhill breaking the long moorland skyline. Note also the extensive views across to the Cleveland Hills beyond the rolling fields of the middle distance. *Gently declining, the track crosses a bridge and promptly forks at the site of High Langwith Cross. The right branch heads on towards Kirkby Malzeard, while our route to the left begins a more pronounced descent from the high moor.*

Descending through the heather the day's second lone rowan is passed, and the moor is finally left at a gate above a plantation. Initially a green road, the way heads straight on and is soon overlaid by a surfaced farm road. At a junction at the end, forsake the road turning uphill in favour of a walled track heading down to the left, with a view over to the tall spire of Healey church. *On the edge of the scattered hamlet of Ilton its surface returns,* passing a Wesleyan Chapel of 1876, now converted to a private dwelling.

At the junction by the open green, turn left down the road past the phone box, soon descending sharply to cross Sole Beck. A largely redundant footbridge waits patiently for a deluge to flood the road. Within a further 50 yards leave by an enclosed track on the left, soon breaking free to run as a lovely green way outside the plantation. At a gate turn up the far side of a solid wall climbing to the derelict farm of High Knowle, and going left in front of the buildings, its drive is found to head through a couple of fields to emerge onto the road to the Druids' Temple.

Returning to the car park, now head through the plantation on a solid track or a green pathway, returning by the other one when the temple and its environs have been fully explored. Numerous other stone edifices are also spread about the woods. The Druids' Temple is a folly for which the eccentric British have long been famous. It was constructed as recently as 1820 by William Danby of Swinton Hall, who thought it a useful way of employing his men. Oval in shape, the inner depths lead to a nodule hiding the 'Tomb'. The full complement of standing stones are based on the rather better known and more historic Stonehenge, though no-one can deny this its own impressiveness. Certainly it exudes quite an atmosphere any day, but particularly if you should have the place to yourself on a wilder day.

The Druids' Temple, Ilton

START Kirkby Malzeard   Grid ref. SE 235743

DISTANCE 7 miles

ORDNANCE SURVEY MAPS
1:50,000
Landranger 99 - Northallerton & Ripon
1:25,000
Explorer 26 - Nidderdale

ACCESS Start from the village centre: ample parking on the main street. Infrequent bus service from Ripon. Galphay and Winksley are served less regularly.

This amble round villages above the river Laver is free of crowds, entirely rural, and visits some interesting buildings and places.

Kirkby Malzeard is an attractive street village once of great importance. The Lordship of Mashamshire was granted to Roger de Mowbray, whose father came over with the Conqueror: his great castle occupied a prominent knoll in the adjacent wooded glen. He fought the Scots at the Battle of the Standard in 1138, and Crusades in the Holy Land: he also founded Byland Abbey, where he spent his twilight years. The castle was destroyed after being besieged during a rebellion against Henry II.

A market charter was granted to John de Mowbray by Edward I in 1307, and the replacement buttercross of 1868 occupies the appropriate site at the village centre crossroads. For centuries after the Conquest, Kirkby Malzeard was the administrative centre of a vast area. The important market and fairs were a major attraction, and the monks of Fountains and Byland came by way of several moorland roads from their Nidderdale estates. One of two surviving inns celebrates the unique achievement of one Henry Jenkins, born in 1500 and who supposedly lived for an astonishing 169 years.

☐ *Leave the cross by turning along the Ripon road. Set back on the left is the rather grand Mowbray House, beyond which is the Fountains Dairy, a source of local cheese. Within a couple of minutes Creets Bridge is reached.* First, note the proud gateposts on the left, with coats of arms and a fine driveway running back alongside attractive woodland. *Over the bridge, turn right along the drive to Lawnwith Farm. Immediately before the first building turn left into the yard, then at once right to pass THROUGH an open barn and out the other side. Cross the field to the left-hand of two gates, continuing up the field-side and along another on the top side of a wood. At the end the centre of an intervening ploughed field must be crossed.* During research this proved impassable, thus resorting to the welcoming pasture to the right.

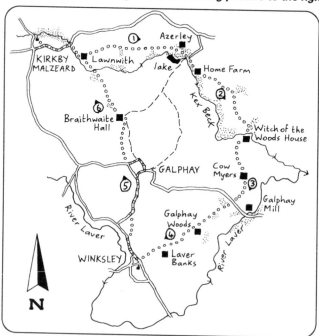

At the far end sanity returns in the more appealing surrounds of Azerley Park, and a fence is followed away towards a building in view in the trees at Azerley. At the bottom swing right to the right-hand of two gates, entering woodland. Fork immediately *right here on a supreme green pathway through the woods in the company of Kex Beck. At the end the road into Azerley is met at a cottage: cross straight over and along the drive past Azerley Grange to Home Farm. The track continues along the yard-side and runs on for a considerable time, largely between hedgerows. Ignoring left turns to Azerley Tower and then Eight Acre Wood, the track drops noticably. As two hedgerows head away, leave the track to the right-hand one, and opt for the pathless left-hand one (a waymark is unlikely to be spotted). Along the top side of a field, it drops to the bottom corner - don't take the stile into the wood, but turn down to cross to a footbridge on Kex Beck.*

The Witch of the Woods House

In the field beyond is the Witch of the Woods House, bizarrely secreted in a pocket of wood. Though first impression is of only a ruinous barn, at the other side of the enclosure stiles lead within: a snatched glance through the window reveals a simply furnished room, complete with a set table - mysterious indeed! Head directly away from the stile and then bear left up to the fence. A gate in it sees our way run left up the other side, through another gate and straight on to Cow Myers Farm. Head between the buildings and out along its surfaced drive onto the Galphay-Ripon road above Galphay Mill and the river Laver.

Cross straight over and along the drive to Galphay Woods. Through lovely park-like grounds high above the river Laver, the drive runs on: a short way before reaching the house, leave by a gate on the right (ineffectively waymarked from the other side) and follow the opposite side of the hedge along a ploughed field-side. At the top a short enclosed way leads to a nicer field, where horse-riders are requested to stay on the track, an informal diversion from the right of way. This runs left and then up the field-side through a gateway, rising up to another gate before swinging left to Laver Banks Farm. Pedestrians can, from the last gate before the farm, continue up the field-side to the brow above the farm, along the field-top to rejoin the track, now a drive, at a cattle-grid. Ahead is the massive tower of Winksley church, and the drive leads down to enter the village.

The church of St Cuthbert & St Oswald (1917, on the site of a chapel built by Abbot Huby, of nearby Fountains) is just along to the left, while the Countryman inn is down the lane just before it. Winksley also has a caravan/camping site. The route turns right along the lane, and out of the village. Heading away between hedgerows, a short-cut of the road corner can be made by taking a gate on the right just before the road swings left into trees. An invisible and clearly unused path runs to the field corner, over a brow and then down, bearing right to find a hurdle which leads to following a hedge away to the Galphay road just short of a barn. Go right into the village. This is a hugely attractive village centre, its spacious green sporting a tall maypole, and a stream tinkling through a smaller, lower green.

Braithwaite Hall

Turn up past the Galphay Inn to a sharp bend, where the drive to Braithwaite Hall is a public path. The impressive gates ask to be used, but an alternative goes left on the road a short way, there taking a stile on the right at a junction. Another invisible path runs on through the park grounds, parallel with the drive but pleasanter. Beyond a miry pond it swings right to rejoin the drive at a cattle-grid to enter the inner grounds, with farm buildings along to the left. Take the main drive ahead, curving left down to the front of the hall. Architecturally very characterful, its great roof appears to entirely overburden the poor stone walls beneath.

Immediately in front turn sharp right, as the drive heading away quickly transforms into a short-lived green way. At the end take the right-hand gate to enter a large sheep pasture. With the tower of Kirkby Malzeard church in view ahead, keep near the left-hand fence to descend the field to a corner gate. Through it, an access track is joined to lead back over Kex Beck to Lawnwith and its drive onto the road. The direct conclusion returns by the outward route, noting, after the dairy, a dark snicket leading into a corner of the churchyard. The church of St Andrew was largely rebuilt after a severe fire in 1908: a Norman doorway remains. It is surrounded by some very old gravestones. If the door is locked a key can be obtained locally.

Kirkby Malzeard

85

18

DALLOWGILL

START Dallow   Grid ref. SE 203713

DISTANCE 6¾ miles

ORDNANCE SURVEY MAPS
1:50,000
Landranger 99 - Northallerton & Ripon
1:25,000
Explorer 26 - Nidderdale

ACCESS The moorland road from Pateley Bridge to Kirkby
Malzeard crosses a cattle-grid to become confined just above
the hamlet of Dallow and before reaching the *Drovers Inn* (a
possible alternative start for patrons). Above the grid there are
several suitable pulling off points on the moorland verges.

☐ *Cross the grid and drop the few yards to a junction. Turn left
along the 'no through road', past farm buildings. The lane loses its
surface at Bowes Farm, but keep on the access road to Dallow.
Press on through the hamlet - above the row of cottages - and the
track runs on above a plantation. When a fork goes left keep
straight ahead to run outside the top of the plantation, until the
track enters it at a gate and descends steeply to South Gill. Cross
by a white footbridge at a ford, then turn right to a similar situation
at the larger North Gill. From the bridge a forest road climbs steeply
to the right, leaving the trees and rising up to meet the Dallowgill
road by the drive to Glebe Farm.*

*At the preceding corner before the road, however, go through a
gate in the fence on the left, and cross the field to a gate into the
woods. Now a superb green bridleway runs along the wood-top,
in springtime enjoying delightful bluebell surrounds. Narrowing
into a nettle-infested squeeze above a plantation, the way*

quickly improves again to reach a hand-gate at the far end. Now below Grey Green Farm, continue along the wall-top through the fields to Bents House, and from a gate keep on over two more fields to the buildings ahead. This is a long-derelict farm, and here turn right up its now grassy drive to rise to an open moor road.

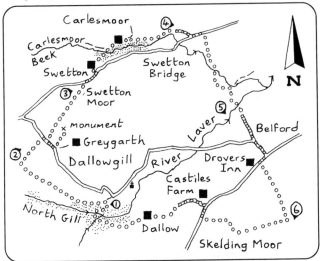

Go right to the cattle-grid, and while the route turns up the near side onto the moor, first make the short detour over the grid to a junction with the lane to Greygarth Methodist Chapel in the farming hamlet. On the left is a stile, and a signpost indicates the detour to Greygarth Monument, up through a stony pasture. The monument was erected to commemorate Queen Victoria's Diamond Jubilee in 1897, and restored in 1984 by the local councils. Inside, an aluminium step-ladder leads to a viewing platform. A modern litter bin was overflowing on our visit - where do people come from with all this rubbish?

This outstanding vantage point reveals great sweeps of moor-land, from those we are fringing to the distant line of the Hambleton and Cleveland Hills of the North York Moors on the eastern horizon. Northernmost of these is the prominent peak of Roseberry Topping, diminutive but unmistakable. At our feet is the cluster of buildings of Greygarth, in the midst of mile upon mile of pastoral country richly interspersed with woodland.

Retrace steps to the stile, and thence to the cattle-grid back onto the moor. Turn up on to the moorland on the right, rising by the wall to the top of Greygarth Hill. Now just over the wall from the monument(!), this is the same superb vantage point. Advance further to descend with the wall, and when it turns away continue down through the heather and rough grass of Swetton Moor to rejoin the road.

At the Greygarth Monument

Drop down the verge to a cattle-grid, and just beyond turn down a farm drive to Swetton on the left. Entering the yard go right to a pair of gates admitting to the top corner of a plantation. A path heads away, dropping pleasantly to cross Carlesmoor Beck by a wooden footbridge. A small waterfall tumbles just downstream.

Rising half-right up the wooded bank a path leaves the trees at a stile to join a track just yards above. Turn right in front of the farm buildings and along the rough lane, passing a house with names carved above the doorway two centuries ago.

The scattered grouping of Carlesmoor is passed before bearing right down a concrete road for a long and pleasant walk, noting en route a three-arched aqueduct in the trees - the water authority asks you not to abseil. A chirpy stream provides company before **the lane eventually rises onto the road we left earlier.** Note the mis-spelt 'Carlsmoor' sign, and pleasing open views to the south over Carlesmoor Beck.

Crossing the river Laver

Go left up to the brow and then branch right down the inviting, hedgerowed green way of Drift Lane to descend to a ford and footbridge on Carlesmoor Beck. This tranquil corner is one to linger over: note the notched gatepost immediately over the bridge, and the abundance of holly in these parts. *Rising to a T-junction, swing left to descend towards the beck. However a sharp turn right sees us on our way again, skirting a wet section before reaching another ford and footbridge, this time over the youthful river Laver* in similarly delightful surroundings.

A steep climb ensues past Low Bellford and up onto the winding road into Dallowgill. Head straight up, however, to meet the Pateley Bridge-Kirkby Malzeard road just a short way below the Drovers Inn.

89

A short-cut turns up past the hostelry - which is well worth a visit in any case, though is normally closed on midweek lunchtimes in winter - to return to the cattle-grid. From the junction by the pub, however, go left a few yards then up initially cowbound Westhod Lane, which part-way returns to superior green status to arrive at a corner of Skelding Moor.

The Drovers Inn, Dallowgill

Through the gate turn immediately right and along the moor edge on a reasonable way, and at the end keep straight on through a gate and across a field. Bear right at the end to a gate in the far wall to return to open moor, and a very colourful corner. Bear right, remaining near the wall which curves around, later finding a trod or two in the heather to run up to meet the moor road just above the cattle-grid.

SKELL GILL

START Skell Gill Bridge   Grid ref. SE 189686

DISTANCE 6½ miles

ORDNANCE SURVEY MAPS
1:50,000
Landranger 99 - Northallerton & Ripon
1:25,000
Explorer 26 - Nidderdale

ACCESS At Skell Gill Bridge on the Pateley Bridge-Kirkby Malzeard road there is room for the odd car, but better space on the road above, on the Pateley side between junction and cattle-grid.

☐ *From the attractive environs of the bridge, climb up the Pateley side and keep on the past the junction. This is likely to have been the course of Pateley-gate, a 12th century moorland crossing to Kirkby Malzeard. Crossing the cattle-grid the road is followed for a few minutes only, before turning left on an unsurfaced lane. Between a sizeable moor and a string of fields this Roman-style way rises to a modest brow - with views to the Brimham Rocks skyline to the right - then runs on to meet the Pateley-Ripon road. Go left a few minutes to a junction with the Brimham Rocks road, then leave the road by a surfaced farm road on the left (signposted Smaden Head Farm shooting ground).*

In the second field, level with a small covered reservoir, leave the farm road by striking right along a sheeptrod: this runs to a gate, then a faint, green track forms to runs along the broad rigg in a straight line descending to Brim House Farm, ahead. Go right at the bottom, through a gate (past old railway vans labelled for pig nuts and cow cake) and onto the farm drive. Leave almost at once however by a stile on the left immediately after the barns.

91

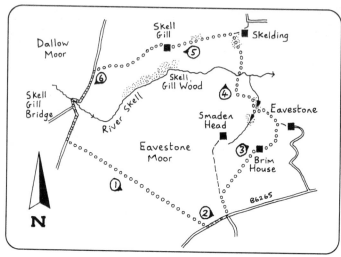

Descend a slim enclosure to a gate at the bottom, from where a green way runs down the field-side. At the bottom take the left of three gates, to follow the left side of a fence down to meet a cart-track visible ahead. Off-route, along to the right is the hamlet of Eavestone.

Skell Gill Bridge

Go left along this pleasant way, soon skirting the enclosure of Brim Bray Pond and rising up to the start of a green lane. In mixed condition this runs along a short way, and when the track swings left to rise to the cluster of barns at Topham Close, turn right, descending the field-side with a stream.

Ahead now is a fine prospect of the side-valley of Skell Gill, which we are about to cross. These are the upper reaches of the river Skell, here seen in very contrasting surroundings to its elegant glide through the parkland of Studley Royal at Fountains Abbey, only a few miles downstream (see WALK 22). At the bottom take a stile on the right and head a few yards downstream before a stile in a fence finds a sturdy footbridge by which to cross the infant Skell.

Skell Gill

Going downstream a few yards further, a stile sees a slim path work up through bracken and brambles: good stuff, but not if wet and too overgrown, in which case an alternative path climbs the field to the left. Throughout are smashing views back over the route and up this secluded private valley. *At the top the enclosed and open ways meet and advance to a gate, from where an enclosed track runs up through new plantings to emerge onto a concrete farm drive.*

Turn left for another direct march, retaining excellent views over the gill to the moors behind. *Passing Crag House the drive approaches the appropriately named Skell Gill Farm at the end. Without entering its confines, go right along a short track before a stream, which crosses it to a gate to a field behind the farm. Cross straight over to a gate in the opposite wall* (this won't budge, so be grateful you've not brought your horse) *to emerge onto the open moor.*

This is trackless, but panic not as the road is not distant, so you can't go far wrong. Bear left towards the wall and only when it kinks for the first of two bends, keep straight on up through the heather to quickly reach the open road - a good guide is a shooters' track coming down to the opposite side of the road. Turn left along ample green verges to conclude, noting a sign telling us where we can't go, but none to say where we can, where our bridleway met the road!

Heather burning on Dallow Moor

94

(20)

EAVESTONE LAKE

START Sawley   Grid ref. SE 248677

DISTANCE 5 miles

ORDNANCE SURVEY MAPS
1:50,000
Landranger 99 - Northallerton & Ripon
1:25,000
Explorer 26 - Nidderdale

ACCESS Start from the expansive green-cum-playing fields, with ample parking alongside. Sawley has a very infrequent bus service from Ripon.

☐ *From the green walk back through the village between the church of St Michael and All Angels (dating from 1879 but on the site of a chapel built by Abbot Huby, of Fountains) and the Sawley Arms to a T-junction. Here take a stile in the facing wall, and head away across the field, bearing gently away from the road over to the left. From a gate at the other side, head away with a hedge on the left. Half-way along, bear right to locate a stile in a holly hedge corner. Aim for the house ahead, joining its drive to approach it.*

On the left is Lacon Hall, its mullioned windows part of an attractive frontage largely hidden to the south. Dating from the 16th century, it replaced an earlier timber hall of the once influential Lacon family. *Pass between the buildings: at a gate cross a small paddock and a tiny beck then rise up the near-side of a wall to a plantation at the top.* This faint path shows signs of causeying, being distinctly raised in parts and therefore clearly of some age and importance.

Look back for a last view of the hall, and far across the Vale of Mowbray to the Hambleton Hills horizon. *From a stile at the top corner, cross diagonally to a similar corner, passing Lacon Cross.*

This wayside cross on its solid base is hollowed at the top, and dates from monastic times, when it was astride a route west from nearby Fountains Abbey towards Nidderdale. **At the corner a stile admits onto the short-lived but well named Green Lane. Go right to emerge into a vast field.** *A near-comprehensive surround of plantations is surprisingly non-claustrophobic.* **Aim across the field, bearing a little right of the one visible farmhouse amid the green fields opposite. Locate a small gate admitting to the plantation in front.**

A broad track slants down to the right to a junction with a forest road. A few yards to the right it runs to an attractively sited lake at a stone hut. **Our route, however, heads left a few yards to descend from the forest road to cross the ancient and remarkably overgrown Butterton Bridge.** *After the causeyed path and Lacon Cross, this is the third successive evidence of this centuries-old route.* **A smashing green path heads away, rising away from the beck above a smaller side beck.** *For the most part a splendid old sunken way rises below a collapsed old wall, before reaching another gate out of the woods. Rise left of a ruined barn to a*

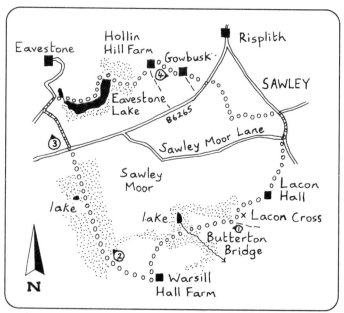

96

gateway, then head up the field-side to a gateway at the top corner. From it rise diagonally to locate a wall-stile to the right of the farm buildings of Warsill Hall, just short of the field corner.

Turn right, away from the farm on a wall-side track towards the impending plantations. Past a near plantation corner keep the same line, with the realisation that the great sweeps of plantation must surely envelop us before long. Back to the right the Hambleton Hills skyline seems only a stone's throw away. *When the track finally leaves the wall to cross a field, keep with the right-hand wall to the plantation corner. From a gate an enclosed way runs inside the plantation boundary to join a forest road running on through the heart of the plantation.*

This runs straight as a die, ignoring branches other than one on the left by a pair of huts, where a tiny deviation incorporates another lovely pond, a great contrast to the harsh forest. Another track leads back to the main drag, which rises gently to leave the plantation. A vague track then runs on outside the boundary wall. Leaving the trees behind, big views return with Kirkby Malzeard Moor prominent on the skyline over to the left. *Dropping to a road junction, cross over and down the Eavestone cul-de-sac.*

From this field-side road note the great pair of boulders sat by the lane up to the left above the farm ahead. **Down past the farm,**

as the road swings sharply to the left, descend a little then take a path that doubles back into the wood. Here begins a glorious short mile, a brilliant little path in the magnificent surround- ings of Eavestone Lake. **First feature is the upper reservoir, with a dark crag jutting out into the water.** This area was a late developer as a climbing ground, but the gritstone surrounding these two lakes now yields climbs of every standard on at least sixteen separate buttresses: some of these literally overhang our path by the main lake!

Lacon Cross

97

The upper lake at Eavestone

Crossing its outflow the path winds round to the head of Eavestone Lake, along which it runs the full length. Of immediate interest are the forbidding outcrops of Ravens Crag towering, often in shadow, above the opposite bank. Waterfowl in abundance, luxuriant foliage and a first-class path all add to the loveliness. The mixed woodland through which we amble is in marked contrast to the dark plantations opposite.

At the end the path crosses a small dam and a lovely little arched bridge. Penance for such delights rears its head in the form of a sustained direct pull through Fishpond Wood, the path winding teasingly from left to right. A gate at the top consigns the Eavestone scene to memory, as an invisible path runs left to join the drive to Hollin Hill Farm. Take its drive all the way round to the back, and go through a gate into a field. Keep to the right beyond some bushes to find a ladder-stile into a slim enclosure. As it opens out keep with its right side to run along to West Gowbusk. Go straight through the farmyard and out along the drive, but quickly leave by a private-looking gate on the left to the front of a cottage at Gowbusk, and follow this drive out onto a lane. Go left a few yards only and take a gate on the right: the houses of Sawley now appear ahead.

Cross the field to a stile in the far corner, then rise gently along the field-side. Enjoy broad views across to the North York Moors, noting also the prominent spire of Studley Royal church and

perhaps a glimpse of the tower of Fountains Abbey in the rolling country ahead. *Upon entering an enclosed rough lane, leave at once by a stile on the left at a concrete hut, and descend the field-side. A stile at the bottom admits to a luxuriant hedgerowed green byway. Short-lived, a stile at the end sends us down the field-side - past a former schoolhouse (a recent casualty, the bell remains in place) - to re-enter the top end of the village green.*

At the foot of Eavestone Lake

START Markington   Grid ref. SE 287649

DISTANCE 5¼ miles

ORDNANCE SURVEY MAPS
1:50,000
Landranger 99 - Northallerton & Ripon
1:25,000
Explorer 26 - Nidderdale

ACCESS Start from the main street; ample roadside parking towards the eastern end. There is also a car park by the village hall, though this is for cricket club use. Occasional bus service from Harrogate (the infrequent 'back' route to Pateley Bridge).

This mild-mannered country ramble - expect some mud - is built around the very major highlight of a close encounter with a magnificent building, off the beaten track but well worth the trek.

☐ *From the village hall go west along the main street past the* Yorkshire Hussar *inn, and turn right along the road for Fountains Abbey. Immediately after crossing Markington Beck (with the mid-19th century parish church of St Michael the Archangel just ahead) bear right along a drive to a lone house, past which a kissing-gate admits to the cricket field. Bear left past the pavilion to another kissing-gate behind a pair of huts. Head away up the hedge-side to a gate at the end, from where a track bears right to run around to Waterloo Farm.*

Pass along the front of the buildings but without actually setting foot on the road, turn left up a short snicket to a stile into a deeply enclosed way, rising as a superb, hollowed way into woodland. Keep straight on to emerge onto a narrow lane in front of a house. Just up to the left, worth a look from the lane, is the impressive *frontage of Ingerthorpe Hall. **The route, meanwhile, goes right a few yards to take a neat old stile in the wall, crossing the field to approach the farm at Yarrows Hill, ahead.** Over to the right the Hambleton Hills form a distant skyline. **In the yard, keep left of all buildings and bear left up to a gate. Note that several gates on this walk are less than keen to open. Cross the field-side to***

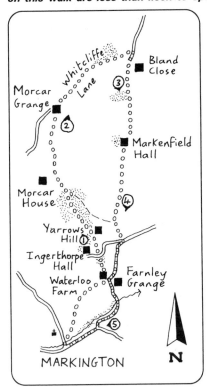

another, and similarly on to reach a junction of tracks, now enveloped by new plantations. Keep straight on again, until faced by further plantings which might shortly block the right of way entirely. A stile is provided, but with no accommodation for a path. Unless trees are removed at some stage, the easier option will be to bear right along the more inviting green way to join the narrow course of Strait Lane a little earlier than planned.

Turn left along this slim bridleway densely lined by foliage, an enjoyable length of which ends all too soon where a stile indicates arrival of the threatened footpath. Emerging into a field keep straight on along the side. Now savour spacious views over this rolling country falling to the vale.

Over to the left behind Morcar House Farm is a prominent tower on the distinctive knoll of How Hill. Now in the care of the National Trust, it replaced a chapel known as Michael-how-Hill that was built by the industrious Abbot Marmaduke Huby of nearby Fountains Abbey. It was already recorded as ruinous two centuries ago.

The Gatehouse, Markenfield Hall

At the field corner, with the church spire of Studley Royal directly ahead, keep on through bridle-gates with Morcar House Farm over to the left. After crossing a stream bear right across the next field to a similar gate. Go left along the field-side, and from the gate at the end bear right again. On this modest brow one absorbs a particularly strong sense of space, with a substantial moorland skyline over to the left, and the more distant line of the North York Moors over to right: splendid stuff. *Descend through a gate and follow the farm track round to Morcar Grange, emerging through the yard onto narrow Whitcliffe Lane. Turning right, this remains our way for some time, soon losing its surface as it runs through this archetypal rolling landscape. Eventually it rises to meet a narrow lane on a brow.*

Turn right, but not before glancing down to the left to see the city of Ripon: sat uneasily amidst its small community is the Cathedral, its light stone partly obscured when trees are in full summer greenery. *The drive runs to the large farm at Bland Close, but from the cattle-grid remain on the hedge-side, through the fields to rise to the brow ahead. On the brow, advance as far as the end of the wood on the right, where a hoary old stile in the ancient 'park wall' leads over a stream into the corner of a large field. Ahead now is the impressive silhouette of Markenfield Hall.* If the field looks unappealing, an alternative bridleway remains outside the wall until reaching a gate below the house, from where a pleasant green way crosses to join the drive, lower down. *Rising to the hall, a track forms to approach it by way of a stile by a gate.* This is a stupendous moment, as it runs by the hall to reveal the moated splendour of the place. Note also from this side the great east window of the chapel.

Markenfield Hall is a fortified manor house dating from 1310. For so long the home of the Markenfield family, Sir Thomas saw an end to that when he played a major role in the Rising of the North in 1569: when this floundered he fled abroad, and the estate was forfeited, eventually passing to Lord Grantley. Another member of the family, Sir Ninian Markenfield, had fought at Flodden Field in 1513. A chapel in Ripon Cathedral recalls the family, with fine tombs dating from the 14th and 15th centuries.

Emerging onto its drive, turn right to the entrance to the hall, and gaze with awe at the magnificent scene. Fronted by a working farm, this is still very much a home. In front is the 16th century gatehouse guarding the bridge over the moat, where a lone black swan dabbled on my visit. The hall is open to the public on a very limited basis, namely Mondays only (closed lunchtime), April to October. Happily much can be seen from outside, but for the modest entry charge it is certainly worth a fuller appraisal if arriving on the right day. The excellently preserved interior includes a fine banqueting hall and the chapel, a good deal of restoration work having taken place in recent times.

Back on the drive, advance a few more yards then take a gate on the left before a set of pens, and follow a track away across the fields. A short enclosed section precedes a final field with a nursery at the end. There a stile admits back onto Strait Lane, at the point where it begins its long narrow section. Here go left, however, along its broad beginnings alongside the nursery to emerge onto a road. Turn right, and if not taking the immediate lane right to return by the outward route, remain on the road past Waterloo Farm and the extensive Farnley Grange to return to the village. The beck is crossed in a particularly endearing setting, deep in woodland where snowdrops proliferate.

The road climbs past the grounds of Markington Hall to re-enter the village. A 17th century manor house, two great wings protrude, with numerous mullioned windows in amongst newer ones. **Turn right along the road from which the hall can be fully appraised, passing the Cross Keys to conclude.**

Markington Hall

22

FOUNTAINS ABBEY

START Fountains Abbey   Grid ref. SE 272686

DISTANCE 5 miles

ORDNANCE SURVEY MAPS
1:50,000
Landranger 99 - Northallerton & Ripon
1:25,000
Explorer 26 - Nidderdale

ACCESS Start from the National Trust car park at Fountains Abbey Visitor Centre off the B6265 Ripon-Pateley Bridge road (served by occasional buses from Ripon). There is an entry fee to the abbey for non-members (keep your ticket safe as the walk leaves and re-enters the grounds). Fountains Abbey is served by bus from the Leeds/Bradford area on Summer Sundays.

The abbey is open daily from 10.00am, except Christmas Eve, Christmas Day, and Fridays in January, November and December.

Fountains Abbey and Studley Royal bear the prestigious World Heritage Site designation: though the walk isn't demanding, the need to savour the wonders of this place certainly is. Don't pencil it in for a half-day! Amongst various literature on sale at the centre, two modestly priced leaflets depict the layout and the history of the abbey itself, and the spacious grounds and their many features.

☐ *From the visitor centre take the main signposted path leading down towards the abbey. It descends a wooded bank to join the main carriageway through the grounds. First feature of interest, and a major one in its own right, is Fountains Hall just to the right. With its intricate facade the magnificent hall was completed in 1611, much of the stone coming from the abbey that had only been abandoned in 1539. Last private owners were the Vyner family, descendants of the Aislabies (mentioned shortly) and much evidence of their presence is found here - note a particularly touching memorial in the hall entrance stairway.*

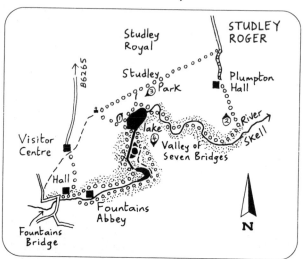

Back on the main carriageway, go left to explore the staggeringly beautiful and most extensive Cistercian remains in England. *Fountains Abbey was founded in 1132 by a group of dissatisfied Benedictine monks from St. Mary's Abbey in York. Seeking a stricter routine, they turned to the French Cistercian order. Though it would have been a much wilder place then, the setting they chose could be matched perhaps only by Bolton and Rievaulx. Built largely between the mid 12th and 13th centuries, this was one of the most important religious houses in the land. Whilst their granges occupied much of nearby Nidderdale, their possessions stretched to the Cumberland fells. Dairy farming, lead mining and other industry also came within their scope, and many ordinary peoples' lives revolved around the abbey. Perhaps its finest feature is the 300ft long west range, with the remarkable vaulted cellarium. Most impressive, however, is the 180ft high tower, a 16th century addition by Abbot Marmaduke Huby.*

Rejoin the main carriageway again. *Scars on the left reveal evidence of quarrying for the great building programme.* **Surfaced throughout, the drive provides a smashing walk along to the water**

gardens, regarded, once again, as the finest in the country. Since the Trust's takeover of the estate from the local authority in the early 1980s, these superb gardens have been subject to an extensive restoration programme, and once again resemble the beautiful scene created throughout the 1700s by the new owners, the Aislabie family. All the buildings such as the temples and the Octagon Tower were also added during this period.

The Temple of Piety across the Moon Pond: Neptune's statue featuring

*Beyond a bend above Half Moon Pond, running above the canalised Skell, we are treated to views over the Moon Pond, flanked by crescents and with lead statues in attendance, to the Temple of Piety: high above, meanwhile, are other features for the return journey. **At the eastern end of the grounds, another shop sees us out past a ticket office to emerge at the lake and the Studley Royal deer park. Here also is a cafe and toilets.***

Follow the drive alongside the lake** - rich with waterfowl - **and at the end fork right on a track to the foot. Here begins the walk through the Valley of the Seven Bridges, the first being a wooden

107

*one over the outflow. Look back from here to see the spire of St. Marys church silhouetted high above the deer park. **The Skell is accompanied downstream through the encroaching walls of this steep-sided valley, a delightful amble that re-crosses the river on five further occasions, each by means of identical stone arched bridges. After the last one the estate is vacated, temporarily, at a tall, deer-proof kissing-gate. A woodland path runs on to pass the seventh bridge** (a plain structure that is not crossed) **before the track climbs the wooded bank to leave the river. Out of the trees it runs a pleasant field-side course with open views.***

In the Valley of the Seven Bridges

Passing the mellow-walled Plumpton Hall and attendant farm buildings, the track becomes surfaced to reach the edge of Studley Roger at a lodge. Here go left along the estate drive, passing through the East entrance arch to re-enter the deer park. Stroll happily along the broad driveway, with St Mary's church framed exquisitely beyond the long avenue of trees. This was laid out to look back to a similarly framed Ripon Cathedral. In the heart of the centuries-old deer park many of these creatures can be discerned, the three breeds present being red deer, fallow deer (most numerous) and Sika deer, introduced from Manchuria in the 1600s. Beyond the deer park is the site of Studley Royal, the house destroyed by fire in 1946 and only stables remaining.

108

When cars are sent left to the car park above the lake, either go with them, or incorporate a visit to the church by remaining on the drive. St Marys was built in 1871-78, boasting an impressive spire prominent throughout the district. It is open to the public only in Easter week and from May to September. *From the church a path descends to the East entrance to the abbey by the lake.*

Re-entering, turn immediately left and cross the Skell as it enters the lake, either by footbridge or stepping stones. The path heads back alongside the water gardens, but just before reaching the Temple of Piety, a higher level alternative offers itself. Slanting back up, pass through the Serpentine Tunnel to emerge by the Octagon Tower. This provides good views over the Moon Pond and much of the grounds. *Continuing, the broad path runs on past the Temple of Fame to the Surprise View at Ann Boleyn's Seat.* The surprise at this wooden shelter is the sudden return of the abbey to the scene, in dramatic style beyond a length of the river. *Just past here the path doubles back down the wooded bank to rejoin the lower one at Half Moon Pond. Turning left the way runs on by the river to return to the abbey, passing Robin Hood's Well en route.* One can turn down to the the ruins for more exploration, or stay on the path above the abbey to arrive at a new museum with a refreshment kiosk. From here the path returns to join the outward carriage-way.

*Fountains Abbey
from the Skell*

LOG OF THE WALKS

WALK	DATE	NOTES (companions, weather, wildlife etc)
1		
2		
3		
4		
5		
6		
7		
8		
9		
10		
11		

LOG OF THE WALKS

WALK	DATE	NOTES (companions, weather, wildlife etc)
12		
13		
14		
15		
16		
17		
18		
19		
20		
21		
22		

INDEX

Principal features (walk number refers)